Teaching Literacy
to Students With
Significant Disabilities

*To children and youth with significant disabilities
who would so like to be considered literate.*

Teaching Literacy
to Students With
Significant Disabilities

Strategies for the K–12

Inclusive Classroom

June E. Downing

CORWIN PRESS
A SAGE Publications Company
Thousand Oaks, California

For information:

Corwin Press
A Sage Publications Company
2455 Teller Road
Thousand Oaks, California 91320
E-mail: order@corwinpress.com

Sage Publications Ltd.
1 Oliver's Yard
55 City Road
London EC1Y 1SP
United Kingdom

Sage Publications India Pvt. Ltd.
B-42, Panchsheel Enclave
Post Box 4109
New Delhi 110 017 India

Printed in the United States of America

Library of Congress Cataloging-in-Publication Data

Downing, June, 1950-
Teaching literacy to students with significant disabilities: strategies for the K-12 inclusive classroom / June E. Downing.
    p. cm.
Includes bibliographical references and index.
ISBN 0-7619-8878-5 (cloth) — ISBN 0-7619-8879-3 (pbk.)
    1. Students with disabilities—Education—United States. 2. Language arts—Remedial teaching—United States. 3. Inclusive education—United States. I. Title.
LC4028.D694 2005
371.9'0446—dc22

                                        2004022984

This book is printed on acid-free paper.

05 06 07 08 09 10 9 8 7 6 5 4 3 2 1

Acquisitions Editor:	Robert D. Clouse
Managing Editor:	Kylee Liegl
Editorial Assistant:	Jaime Cuvier
Production Editor:	Tracy Alpern
Copy Editor:	Carla Freeman
Proofreader:	Penelope Sippel
Typesetter:	C&M Digitals (P) Ltd.
Indexer:	Sylvia Coates
Cover Designer:	Anthony Paular
Graphic Designer:	Lisa Miller

Contents

Foreword

LITERACY IS LIBERTY

This book would not have been written just 10 years ago. If it had been written, it certainly would not have been published. As June Downing points out in this unique book, literacy considerations for students with significant disabilities are new, novel, and still not commonplace.

You see, students with disabilities have been systematically excused from literacy instruction. Early in the history of special education, students with significant disabilities did not even attend school. When they did, they were educated in segregated schools and classrooms, and their curriculum and instruction were not based on the core curriculum of the school. In fact, students with significant disabilities spent a great deal of their instruction day engaged in isolated skills instruction.

Over the years, and with lots of advocacy from parents and some educators, students with significant disabilities began to spend increasing amounts of time in regular classrooms. Even so, the field did not focus on literacy instruction. As Downing points out, this is likely due to the expectations people had for students who experienced significant disabilities. The field focused on gaining access to general education classrooms, with supports and services. This required significant attention to answering the question of why students with disabilities should be educated with peers without disabilities. Over time and as students with significant disabilities accessed the core curriculum, we began to notice that students were exceeding our expectations. In fact, they were displaying reading, writing, speaking, and listening skills (e.g., Kliewer, 1998; Ryndak, Morrison, & Sommerstein, 1999).

Today the research is clear: Inclusion works. As Downing notes, access to general education classrooms and the core curriculum has become a given in the education of students with significant disabilities. As a result, the field stands prepared to address a most pressing issue: literacy.

June Downing is the perfect person to tackle this pressing need. She has a wealth of knowledge and has been involved with the field of special education as a teacher, researcher, and leader. She is known for her ability to translate complex issues into common practice. She understands the needs, wants, and desires of people with significant disabilities. But most important, she knows that literacy brings liberty. Without providing students with significant disabilities access to the written word, we deny them the world. Said another way, literacy is power—power to control your own life and influence the world around you.

Teaching Literacy to Students With Significant Disabilities: Strategies for the K–12 Inclusive Classroom makes an important contribution. First, Downing challenges the accepted definition of literacy. She extends the work of Gallego and Hollingsworth (2000), who challenged the classroom standard of literacy and suggested that there are multiple literacies that students use both in and out of school. Downing extends their conceptualization and the common definition of literacy even further by exploring the various ways that students can and do use information to make meaning of the world.

Second, Downing explores the changes that must be made in the educational system if we are to ensure that "no child is left behind" and that every student really does have access to highly qualified teachers who believe that they can learn. This is no short order. Downing understands that every member of the educational community has a role to play if we are to accomplish this goal. She also provides specific guidelines for us to follow as we begin to provide students with significant disabilities access to literacy instruction.

Literacy instruction is the third area in which Downing makes a substantial contribution. While this book challenges accepted theories and explores the research base, it does so much more than that. This book is practical. Readers—from family members to teachers to related services staff to administrators—will develop and extend their understanding of quality literacy instruction for all students, including those who have historically been left behind. Strategic teaching is important, as we know that "teachers matter and what they do matters most" (Fisher & Frey, 2004, p. 1). In other words, the knowledge, skills, and dispositions of the teachers—general and special education—are likely to be the most important predictors of the success a student has in learning literacy. Again, Downing demonstrates her understanding of this and provides a wealth of information regarding the ways that students can become literate.

The final area in which *Teaching Literacy to Students With Significant Disabilities: Strategies for the K–12 Inclusive Classroom* meets a unique need is in evaluating progress. Too often, general and special educators do not know what to do when students fail to make progress. This book articulates a system of support for teachers and students as we implement instructional plans. This system is clear and will likely result in a laserlike focus on ensuring that students with and without disabilities become literate thinkers who contribute to our society.

In sum, I invite you to read between the lines and infer that this book is unique and important. June Downing has challenged our assumptions about and expectations for students with significant disabilities. She has also provided direction for meeting these new expectations. June clearly believes that all students must participate in regular classrooms with their peers without disabilities and that students with significant disabilities must have access to quality literacy instruction. In fact, nothing less than the freedom and liberty for all of our students depends on it.

Douglas Fisher
Professor of Literacy and Language Education
San Diego State University

Acknowledgments

I am very grateful for the individuals who gave of themselves to make this book come to fruition. I would certainly like to thank Dr. Doug Fisher for agreeing so willingly and quickly to read this book and write the foreword. His knowledge of literacy is well-known in the field, and I was quite thrilled and honored when he said he could do this. I value his work greatly, and his thoughts in the foreword are a very special gift to me. Thank you, Doug.

Photographs always add a great deal to any written work, and I am grateful for those who helped me with the photographs for this book. First, I would like to thank the parents of the children pictured in this text. Showing their children in literacy activities really highlighted what I was trying to say. I appreciate their willingness to share their children with the readers of this book. Second, I would not be able to include the photographs if I hadn't had the support of the photographers. I owe a debt of gratitude to Lauren Etting for taking the pictures of some elementary school-aged children who appear in this text. These children attend a fully inclusive elementary school where Lauren works as a paraeducator. Her photographs are great and really capture early literacy skills as well as the natural support of an inclusive environment. Thank you, Lauren. I also must thank Ben Adams, a friend, colleague, and parent of a child with severe and multiple disabilities, who is also a professional photographer. His photographs of children are a delightful gift to this book. I so value his support and willingness to share this gift.

Other photographs in the book picture adapted materials that can be used to support literacy involvement for students with significant challenges. These photographs were taken by a friend and colleague, Dr. Lavada Minor. Despite her busy schedule, Lavada was always ready to bring her camera from home and work with me to capture images that were explained in the text. Her photographs definitely help clarify what I was trying so hard to describe. I so appreciate her willingness to do this for me.

I certainly owe a debt of gratitude to all of the experts in the field of literacy whose work has helped so many students and their teachers. Their work has added considerably to the information presented in the following pages. I would also like to thank the reviewers of the first draft of this text, even though I have never met them. Their time and careful reading of this manuscript contributed to a much clearer and more detailed version, and I am very grateful for the time and effort they expended. Their comments were very helpful and encouraging.

Many of my students have contributed to the making of this book either directly or indirectly. Their questions in my classes have served as a catalyst for me to explore the area of literacy and address it as well as I could in this book. I hope I challenge them as much as they challenge me. I have asked a few students (who are also teachers) if I could describe some of their accommodations that they have made in this book. I hope they didn't feel as if they had to, but still, their contributions in the form of examples really added to the content. I believe that these examples will help other teachers as well.

I definitely want to acknowledge the support of my clerical assistant during the writing of this book. Nadine Thomas helped me a great deal with most of the figures that appear in this text. She was always eager and willing to track down anything I might need to make the work progress quickly. Her support was certainly welcomed and greatly appreciated.

Finally, I would like to thank the many individuals at Corwin Press who have been involved in the development of this product from its inception. Their efforts to produce materials that support students with disabilities are greatly needed and much appreciated by those of us in the field.

Corwin Press gratefully acknowledges the contributions of the following reviewers:

Robin Greenfield
Professor
University of Idaho, Boise Center
Boise, ID

Julie Van Den Brandt
LD Teacher
Edison Elementary School
Appleton, WI

Victoria Wells, NBCT
Exceptional Needs Specialist
Suwannee Elementary School
Algona, WI

Mary Novak
LD Teacher
Algona Elementary School
Algona, WI

Joan L. Erickson
Associate Professor
College of Education and
  Human Sciences
University of Nebraska, Lincoln
Lincoln, NE

Carrie Carpenter
Teacher
Oregon's 2003 Teacher of the Year
Hugh Hartman Middle School
Redmond, OR

Martha J. Larkin
Author, Professor
Department of Special Education/
  SLPA
State University of West Georgia
Carrollton, GA

About the Author

June E. Downing, PhD, is a professor at California State University, Northridge (CSUN), in the Department of Special Education, where she prepares teachers to work in the area of moderate and severe disabilities. She is a national leader in the field of special education that targets the needs of students with severe disabilities, especially with regard to inclusive education. She has published several articles, chapters, and monographs and three books on students having severe and multiple disabilities. She has received awards in her field, including the Robert Gaylord-Ross Scholarship Award from CalTASH in 1997 and was honored to be named CSUN's Outstanding Professor for 2000. She is currently on the executive board of TASH, an international advocacy organization for individuals with severe disabilities. She is an associate editor of *Research and Practice for Persons with Severe Disabilities* and serves on other professional editorial boards.

Introduction

Students with the most severe types of disabilities often are prejudged as incapable of participating and certainly benefiting from a number of fairly common life activities. The more severe the disability, the more typical is the reaction. Others around these individuals may predetermine that due to physical limitations, sensory impairments, limited cognitive abilities, and minimal communication skills, going places and doing things may not be enjoyed. For instance, it may be assumed that taking a child who is totally deaf and blind with significant other disabilities to the local zoo would not be beneficial to the child. The question, "What is he going to get out of this?" is raised. As a result, the student may miss out on a number of meaningful experiences or miss experiences that could have been meaningful. One of those experiences and the focus of this book is the range of experiences that equate with literacy. Students with severe disabilities have limited access to literacy activities and instruction. They may have had limited access to the many experiences that lay a foundation for literacy activities as well. Given the critical importance of literacy for students' learning, the situation cannot continue to exist.

This book is written specifically for special educators and paraeducators who are responsible for teaching students with severe disabilities, aged preschool through adulthood. Since a basic premise of this book is that students with severe disabilities will be educated in general education classrooms with their peers with no disabilities, the intended audience for this book also includes general educators who will have such students as members of their classes. To fully accept ownership of their students with severe disabilities, general educators, regardless of the grade level they teach, will need to understand how these students can benefit from various literacy activities. The intent of this book is to provide teachers with this information. Of equal importance, this book hopes to support the efforts of parents and family members as they strive to obtain the most effective and meaningful educational program for their children. The information in the following pages is designed to encourage family members to continue their literacy activities with their children and to serve as a catalyst for new activities and experiences that might support their children's learning. Having this information may support them in their advocacy efforts for their children.

Although not the main objective of the text, the information provided strongly supports the movement toward educating students with their same-age peers without disabilities. For the purpose of this text, inclusive education is considered full-time placement in the age-appropriate classroom(s) that the student would attend if not disabled. Physical placement alone is not the goal, but rather the curriculum is adapted and modified to meet the unique needs of each student having a severe disability. Support is provided through highly qualified special educators, trained paraeducators, adapted materials, modified expectations, and a philosophy of acceptance of human differences. This preference for an inclusive educational environment is based on research supporting the benefits for all children (Downing, Spencer, & Cavallaro, 2004; Fisher & Meyer, 2002) and the dearth of research supporting a separate educational system based on ability. In fact, a comprehensive search of the literature for research that demonstrated the effectiveness of a segregated placement as compared with an inclusive placement for students with severe disabilities yielded no such documentation (Falvey, Blair, Dingle, & Franklin, 2000). Therefore one basic assumption of this text is that students of all ages and ability levels are learning together in supported inclusive environments.

In general, the purpose of this text is to highlight literacy instruction for students with severe disabilities and demonstrate the many ways that these students can gain access to literacy activities. To do so, adherence to a strict definition of literacy is not conducive, and a much broader and all-encompassing definition will be used. This book will attempt to offer some suggestions for broadening perceptions of literacy to be more inclusive of all students. Specific strategies and examples are provided throughout the book, which may prove helpful to a number of students. However, each student is unique and will require individualized intervention to be most effective. While just an initial effort, it is hoped that the ideas presented in the following pages will serve to further the literacy movement.

The target population for this book includes those students of all ages who have so frequently been excluded from most literacy experiences. These students typically have a moderate to profound level of intellectual impairment and may have very severe and complex communication challenges. In addition, students are likely to have visual, hearing, and/or physical disabilities. They may have health impairments and behavioral challenges as well. These additional disabilities may be mild or severe. The result of these multiple and complex disorders can make learning quite challenging, although certainly not impossible.

Although the book primarily addresses the needs of this population of students, suggestions for literacy activities and literacy skill development may be equally applicable to a much broader range of students. Furthermore, the examples and strategies suggested in this book target the school day. However, many of these suggestions have application to the home environments and should be implemented there as well. Ideally the ideas presented in this text will encourage the reader to experiment with different literacy experiences and activities with a large number of students who struggle to access and understand their world.

Literacy and a Free Appropriate Public Education

KEY CONCEPTS

- Literacy is for everyone and comes in many different forms.
- Federal mandates support literacy instruction for everyone.
- Several barriers exist that can be overcome concerning literacy instruction for students with severe disabilities.
- Literacy skills enhance one's quality of life in many ways.
- Literacy instruction is as important for students with significant disabilities as it is for everyone.

Literacy may be regarded in myriad ways. Some perspectives of literacy are broad and inclusive in nature, while others are more rigidly defined and exclusive. For example, a strict adherence to the traditional view of literacy as reading print automatically excludes certain students for whom such a skill may never be attained. One might conclude, therefore, that literacy would not be appropriate for such students. What this chapter intends to do is reexamine the definition of literacy and offer a broader definition so that it is most certainly appropriate for *all* students.

WHAT IS LITERACY?

Literacy has been defined as:

> [The] minimal ability to read and write in a designated language, as well as a mindset or way of thinking about the use of reading and writing in everyday life. It differs from simple reading and writing in its assumption of an understanding of the appropriate uses of these abilities within a print-based society. Literacy, therefore, requires an active, autonomous engagement with print and stresses the role of the individual in generating as well as receiving and assigning independent interpretations to messages. (Harris & Hodges, 1995, p. 142)

When the focus is on visual decoding and comprehending the written word, students who have multiple impairments and are unable to visually access print and understand are precluded from engaging in literacy. If literacy instruction is to be confined to recognizing and interpreting very abstract visual symbols, then those students unable to perceive or make sense of such abstraction are automatically excluded.

There are several levels of literacy, however, with emergent skills having applicability to a wide range of students. Emergent literacy skills, such as the recognition that books exist and have meaning, begin at very young ages. Parents regularly read to their young infants. Although the child may not understand what the spoken words represent, these are the first experiences with literacy that lay a strong foundation for the development of advanced literacy skills. The importance of reading to children as a basic building block to literacy has been well documented (Cunningham, 1995; Sulzby, 1994; Sulzby & Teale, 1991). We would not withhold this experience from children simply because they did not have conventional reading skills. Such skills are neither expected of young children nor needed. Reading can be meaningful and pleasurable on many different levels.

A more encompassing view of literacy than one with a strict adherence to the printed word includes listening and speaking and interacting as well as reading, writing, and spelling and, as such, obviously includes everyone. The relationship between literacy and communication will be more fully discussed in Chapter 2 of this text. However, it is imperative to know that everyone communicates, and therefore everyone can engage in literacy experiences (Mirenda, 1993). When we communicate, we often use symbols to convey our meaning. These symbols can be written down, maintained in a permanent format, and read by others. Effective communication is certainly one critical aspect of literacy.

Another way to broaden our thinking about literacy is to reconceptualize how literacy materials can be adapted to be more inclusive. Although everyone may not be able to adequately access print or be able to express themselves via the written word, other formats may help with accessibility. For students with severe cognitive, physical, and sensory impairments, alternatives to written text are essential. In addition to text, these students can read and write using a variety of forms, such as pictures, objects, parts of objects, and textures. Specifics concerning methods of adapting literacy materials appear in Chapter 3 and again in Chapter 4, where they are described within a contextual framework. In general, by expanding literacy activities to include any means of gaining information and in expressing oneself, students with the most severe disabilities are not excluded from these important activities. Literacy is for everyone, and what literacy is should be individually determined for each student with severe disabilities.

LITERACY AND FEDERAL MANDATES IN EDUCATION

Several legislative efforts exist on a national level to support equal educational opportunities for all children. The primary legislation aimed at supporting the educational rights of students having disabilities is the Individuals with Disabilities Education Act (IDEA) of 1990 and its reauthorization of 1997. Through this legislation, students are guaranteed a free and appropriate public education (FAPE) in the least restrictive environment (LRE) with all the necessary supports and services that would enable the student to benefit from the specialized education. While the intent of the law may be clear, its interpretation and implementation for individual students has proved to be quite challenging. Determining an appropriate education for a given child may have less to do with student goals and needs, and more with the expertise, training, and experiences of team members (Giangreco, Edelman, & Dennis, 1991; Lake & Billingsley, 2000). Although no one curriculum could possibly be determined appropriate for all students with disabilities, without a stated appropriate program, extreme variation can occur with what is offered a given student. One educational team could decide that the focus will be on maintaining a student's physical health and safety, while another educational team could decide that a much more academic curriculum is appropriate for the same student. The variability in determining what is appropriate can be significant within a school district and becomes quite pronounced when comparisons are made across states.

In addition to an appropriate education, IDEA clearly states the necessity of ensuring access to the core curriculum for all students. Obviously, the core curriculum entails considerable literacy, with national standards highlighting expected competencies to be attained at different grade levels. The implication is that all students regardless of ability level should be receiving literacy instruction as part of that access to the core curriculum requirement. As with the mandate for appropriate education, however, there is no clear direction provided as to how to ensure access to the core curriculum for those students who do not display conventional literacy skills. Therefore how access to the core curriculum is interpreted also varies widely across student teams, school districts, and states. Furthermore, where a student receives his or her education has a major impact on gaining access to the core curriculum. For example, findings from a study of 33 middle school students with intellectual impairments revealed that they were much less likely to work on tasks related to the core curriculum in self-contained segregated classrooms than in general education classrooms (Wehmeyer, Lattin, Lapp-Rincker, & Agran, 2003). Therefore while the national mandate strongly supports all students accessing the core curriculum with the accompanying high expectations, minimal guidance exists to determine what that might look like for a student with complex and multiple disabilities.

As teachers and family members struggle to determine what an appropriate education is for a given student, valued social outcomes should be considered. Carpenter, Bloom, and Boat (1999) recommend that four socially valid outcomes of self-esteem, self-determination, empowerment, and joy be used to guide education practices. Being literate in today's society strongly supports the attainment of these valued outcomes for all individuals. The manner in which literature is defined by teachers and other team members will need to be broadened so that literacy content and activities are made accessible and appropriate for all students. Then the team can develop an individualized educational program with measurable goals and objectives that reflect what literacy skills will be learned by the student and how the student will demonstrate mastery.

Literacy is considered a critical lifelong skill that serves as a benchmark for future educational and vocational success (Gurry & Larkin, 1999; Kliewer & Landis, 1999). As such, a strong emphasis has been placed on teaching all children to read and write before they leave school. Different federal programs have been implemented with the specific purpose of raising academic expectations for all students, with specific emphasis on improving literacy skills (Goals 2000: Educate America Act, 1994; No Child Left Behind, 2001). Given this importance and the profound impact literacy can play in an individual's life, it is hard to imagine an appropriate educational program for a student with disabilities that does not involve at least some focus on literacy.

As written in 1994, Goals 2000: The Educate America Act targeted specific goals for all students to achieve. The specific goal for literacy stated that every adult would be literate and possess the skills and knowledge to successfully compete in a global economy and exercise the rights and responsibilities of citizenship (Goals 2000: Educate America Act, 1994). This stated goal recognizes the importance of literacy acquisition for all individuals. Unfortunately, this education act did not articulate how every adult would become literate or what exactly being literate meant, especially for students with severe disabilities.

The No Child Left Behind Act (NCLB) of 2001, originally known as The Elementary and Secondary Education Act, provides a legal mandate to ensure that all students are learning and that schools are responsible for that learning. As a component of this law, *Reading First* is a national initiative to train teachers how to promote literacy for all young children. Federal funding has been provided to support this initiative. While the premise of NCLB affirms the value of education and of learning for everyone, certain requirements of this act call into question its applicability to those students who have the most significant disabilities. For example, the requirement that *all* students read at a certain grade level does not seem to take into account those students for whom traditional literacy mastery is not attainable. There are students who, while being quite capable of learning, may not be able to access or understand abstract literacy skills in either print or braille. Does this mean that they are excluded from the No Child Left Behind Act? Does this legislation need to be renamed, or the intent of the law modified and restated?

According to this federal law (NCLB), all teachers must be highly qualified in the subject matter they teach. Unfortunately, the law is not clear on what constitutes "highly qualified" for teachers in special education who teach a variety of subject matter (usually kindergarten through 12th grades). Specific skills that would identify mastery in subject matter for teaching students with severe disabilities have not been delineated. For example, it is not known what skills in literacy instruction would represent a highly qualified educator of students with significant disabilities who do not engage in literacy activities in a conventional manner. What kind of test would educators need to pass to demonstrate competency prior to teaching? According to a national survey to special education directors, not one respondent felt that teachers were well prepared to teach literacy skills to students who were nonverbal (Heller, Fredrick, Dykes, Best, & Cohen, 1999). This is a troubling statistic, since a high-quality teacher is considered the single most important factor in students' learning (Mainger, Deshler, Coleman, Kozleski, & Rodriguez-Walling, 2003).

If NCLB really applies to all students, as its name implies, then efforts must be taken to realize that literacy acquisition may take different forms and involve different instruction for different children. Those creating legislation designed to include all students must be made aware of the diversity expressed by our student population so that they don't inadvertently exclude some. While accountability is a critical issue in education, setting standards that automatically exclude a certain population of students (and their teachers) does not make the mandate inclusive. At the same time, students with the most significant disabilities should be expected to achieve and to make progress toward meaningful goals (Ford, Davern, & Schnorr, 2001). They should not be excluded from high expectations. Different standards that truly apply to all and acknowledge the diversity in our student population are needed. No child should be left behind, and legislation must be carefully written that reflects this philosophy.

BARRIERS TO LITERACY INSTRUCTION FOR STUDENTS WITH SIGNIFICANT DISABILITIES

Several barriers exist to hinder the acquisition of literacy skills for students with significant disabilities. While perhaps unpleasant, these barriers should be addressed so that efforts can be made to circumvent them and focus our energy and time on the process of bringing literacy instruction to those who have been most often deprived of it. Since it is always easier to use a barrier as an excuse for inaction, significant effort will be needed to create avenues around these barriers. The first step may be to recognize that they exist. In the following pages, attention is focused on some of these barriers.

Attitudinal Barrier

Perhaps the greatest barrier is the temptation to place the blame for lack of literacy skills on the child and theorize that the child is too disabled to acquire these skills and cannot benefit from instruction. The belief that literacy was not even an option for certain individuals due to the presence of a disability has been well documented (Barudin & Hourcade, 1990; Fossett, Smith, & Mirenda, 2003; Kliewer, 1998; Locke & Butterfield, 1998). This attitude removes all responsibility from the shoulders of those supporting the child and forces the child to prove the right to access this type of instruction. However, legal mandates make it clear that no child has to prove himself or herself capable of learning. That is assumed. What is required are creative strategies to help the child learn despite disabilities that can make this challenging. Instead of believing that these individuals cannot learn and cannot benefit from literacy activities, we must affirm the opposite and then determine ways to make this possible. The unexpected discovery of literacy skills of individuals having severe disabilities through a systematic prompting strategy known as "Facilitated Communication" stands as testimony to the dangers of presumed incompetence (Kliewer, 1998; Kliewer & Biklen, 2001). See the sidebar for information on this somewhat controversial strategy.

What Is Facilitated Communication?

Facilitated Communication (FC) is an intervention strategy designed to support the communication efforts of individuals who are essentially nonverbal with limited unaided communication (Biklen, 1993; Crossley, 1994). Characteristics of FC include physical support/resistance at the hand, wrist, forearm, elbow, upper arm, or shoulder; emotional support to encourage attempts by the individual; and the expectation that the individual can and will communicate using some type of communication device (e.g., alphabet/word board, computer with keyboard, picture board). While physically supported to control errant movements (e.g., tremors, flailing hands, perseveration on a letter or a word), the individual points to letters, words, and/or pictures to state a message.

The controversy surrounding FC concerns the question of authorship. When individuals first use FC to communicate, physical support/resistance is typically provided at the hand, which raises the concern regarding who actually is creating the message (Green & Shane, 1994). Although the goal of FC is to fade physical support as soon as possible, the concern is that those providing facilitation may, in fact, be manipulating the individual's hand and creating the messages. The somewhat sudden engagement in skilled communicative interactions by individuals who had previously not displayed such purposeful and interactive behavior raises suspicion regarding authorship.

However, a certain degree of influence exists whenever instruction occurs with individuals who require substantial support to learn new skills. Often a student's hands may be physically guided to a device to request assistance when it appears that this is what the student needs. Brown, Gothelf, Guess, and Lehr (1998) question whether it is possible to teach individuals with profound disabilities any skill without at least somewhat influencing their behavior. The intent of FC as a support strategy is never to guide the individual's hand, forcing them to create messages, but rather to follow their movements and provide the necessary physical stability so that they can make use of this technique. As with any intervention strategy, techniques can be improperly applied. However, some individuals using FC as a means of communication have advocated for its continued use (Goddard, 2002), and some research exists to support its continued use as a viable strategy for some individuals (Cardinal, 2002). Using FC with individuals has as its premise the expectation of competence—the belief that all individuals can communicate. In this regard, it is consistent with the premise of this book, that all individuals can and do communicate and can benefit from literacy instruction.

Low Expectations

A familiar partner of negative attitudes is low expectations. Unfortunately, students with the most significant disabilities often face low expectations by those providing care and services. These students are not expected to read or write, and those types of goals may not emerge during educational planning. The emphasis may be on taking care of the student's health care needs, feeding the child, positioning the child, and making sure that the student is safe and clean. While certainly necessary considerations for all children, such "goals" fall far short of our legal mandates to leave no child behind.

When literacy instruction has been considered for students with moderate disabilities, the focus has been on reading "survival" words (Browder & Lalli, 1991; Katims, 2001). Unfortunately, it is difficult to determine what are survival words for individual students who may spend considerable time being drilled on words like *danger, poison,* and *warning* and never really encounter such words in their daily environments. How will mastery of such words improve a student's quality of life, as more meaningful reading can do? Furthermore, unless the student is taught these words when and where they occur, problems with generalization of the skill may make it meaningless. For example, one student known by the author could recognize the words *boys* and *girls* and *men* and *women* consistently when presented on flash cards. However, this same student did not know which restroom to enter and could not recognize these same words on restroom doors. More important, there are more valuable benefits of reading that can lead to a lifetime of personal enjoyment, such as reading through photo albums of past events or flipping through the pages of a favorite magazine.

Students will achieve to our expectations if provided the right type of support. It is imperative, therefore, that we maintain high expectations for *all* children and ensure that we are constantly challenging children to learn. Students with significant disabilities certainly will not acquire literacy skills (and other academic skills) if we do not expect them to or provide them with opportunities to do so. If we perceive them to be incapable of learning, then they may easily meet that expectation. For example, a teacher makes it clear to a paraprofessional to keep books and other reading materials away from a particular student because he will destroy them. Occasionally, the student does get his hands on a book and does proceed to tear it apart. This confirms the teacher's expectations, and she issues a stronger precaution to the paraprofessional to see that this doesn't happen again. No effort is made to understand the student's behavior with the book. Perhaps he wants to read and is frustrated because he can't. Perhaps he recognizes that he is the only student in this class who is not allowed access to reading (and writing) material. Perhaps he has never been taught how to handle a book and the enjoyment that a book can bring. Instead of being denied access to literacy materials, he needs specific instruction in how to make good use of these materials. Without this instruction, he will not have the opportunity to learn what he may most desire. As Katims (2001) states, "We need to overcome our lack of literacy optimism for students with mental retardation" (p. 171). We need to raise both our expectations for these students to read and our expectations for our teachers to teach.

Limited Opportunities

Literacy builds on our life experiences, which is why it is imperative to provide children with multiple experiences to support their learning. Children with severe physical impairments may lack experiential learning due to the difficulty they have walking and physically exploring their environments (Blischak, 1995). When children have significant disabilities that may involve the multiple impact of physical, cognitive, and sensory impairments, the ability to explore and learn from this exploration may be even more hampered. To compound the problem, experiences can become limited as care providers question the value of these experiences. Instead of supporting the child's involvement in varied experiences on an ongoing basis, the decision may be made to keep the child at home, where he or she is most comfortable. Unfortunately, such a decision further handicaps the child, making it more difficult to acquire and understand basic concepts.

The importance of reading to children at home as a strong foundation for literacy skills development has been well supported in the literature (Cunningham, 1995; Sulzby, 1994; Sulzby & Teale, 1991). Yet the amount of time that family members spend reading to a child with a disability, especially a severe disability, is considerably less than the time families spend reading to a child who does not have disabilities (Light & Kelford Smith, 1993; Marvin, 1994). A short attention span or the inability to see pictures, hear words, or respond consistently to these efforts may explain this finding. Perhaps the inconsistent response of these children discourages the parents, causing them not to want to spend much time in such activities. Family members may not have the time to engage in literacy activities as often as other families because they must devote considerable time and attention to meeting basic physical and health needs.

Even at school, students with significant disabilities appear to be overlooked when it comes to literacy opportunities. Several researchers have examined classroom experiences for students with moderate to severe disabilities and have reported minimal opportunities for these students with regard to literacy. Teachers perceived these students as not being sufficiently capable to benefit from literacy activities (Katims, 2001; Kliewer, 1998; Kliewer & Biklen, 2001; Ryndak, Morrison, & Sommerstein, 1999). The emphasis on developing a linear sequence of isolated skills (e.g., letter naming, letter-sound association) before accessing meaningful literacy seemed to keep students from more meaningful literacy instruction (Ryndak et al., 1999).

Limited Means of Accessing Literacy

Even if children with significant disabilities are given the opportunity to engage in literacy experiences, if they do not have the means to interact during these experiences, they cannot demonstrate what they know. Often children with significant disabilities do not have speech or a solid language base, so that sharing experiences, understanding stories, and talking about them are challenging. These children cannot easily interact with others during literacy activities, such as reading a book, due specifically to their disabilities (e.g., pointing to pictures when arms and hands have limited movement due to a severe physical disability). Children with multiple disabilities who are deaf may see the pictures but may be unable to hear the story being read. Their understanding and enjoyment of stories may be greatly reduced as a result.

Parents of children who use augmentative communication devices report having lowered expectations for their children to ever acquire true literacy (Marvin, 1994). Ensuring meaningful access to literacy experiences will be featured in Chapters 3 and 4 of this book and so will not be discussed in depth here. However, the critical need to ensure that children with significant disabilities have a means of active engagement in literacy experiences is a main objective for those supporting these students (Fisher & Kennedy, 2001). Alternate strategies and adapted materials will be needed to help students be meaningfully involved.

Limited Time

One very realistic barrier to literacy learning for students with severe disabilities is the limited time that teachers have to adapt and design appropriate literacy materials for their students. When students are unable to access standard materials used by their peers without disabilities, teachers must create the necessary and often highly individualized material. Special educators must first collaborate with general educators to determine what topics are to be studied and what materials will be used as part of the core curriculum and daily lesson plans. They must then adapt worksheets, book chapters, book report forms, newsletters, and whatever else will be used to improve their students' understanding of the information and to provide them with an appropriate means to demonstrate this understanding.

Considerable time is required to ensure accessibility to the core curriculum, especially for those students with the most significant and complex disabilities. As the content becomes more abstract and is presented at an increasingly fast pace (as in secondary schools), the responsibility of adapting all necessary materials can become overwhelming. The increased number of teachers that need to be involved in this collaborative process at the secondary levels adds to the difficulty. Finding the time to collaborate, plan together, and determine a strategy for meeting individual student needs is essential (Downing, Spencer, & Cavallaro, 2004; Hunt, Soto, Maier, & Doering, 2003). Some suggestions for addressing this dilemma are presented in Chapter 3 of this text. Each educational team will need to determine the most effective means of making literacy accessible given their own unique situation.

The Age Factor

Finally, there is a feeling that if children do not acquire literacy skills by a certain age, then efforts at further literacy activities should not be attempted. Students may end up with a few years in elementary school where they have a chance to demonstrate their literacy skills. Such thinking is evident for students with and without disabilities, so that students who do not acquire reading and writing skills during the elementary years will find themselves without access to specific instruction in these areas in later years. However, some studies of adults have refuted this type of thinking and provided some evidence that it is never too late to open the world of literacy for an individual. Ryndak et al. (1999) demonstrated the development of literacy skills with a high school student after she had been moved from a self-contained setting and placed in general education. Stromer, Mackay, Howell, and McVay (1996) taught an adult with moderate intellectual impairments and a hearing impairment to spell by matching pictures to printed words using a computer and a choice of letters. Brady and McLean (1996) found that some adults with severe mental retardation learned to state the word by reading the accompanying pictorial symbol. Gordon Pershey and Gilbert (2002) were successful in teaching a woman of 35 to gain meaningful literacy skills after 7 years of instruction. They reported that the skills she acquired improved her quality of life by enhancing her enjoyment, increasing her participation, and allowing her to communicate more effectively with others. Teaching meaningful literacy skills is important no matter the individual's age. Determining what to teach and how to do this in a manner that is relevant and interesting to the learner should be the focus, and not the age of the individual.

LITERACY AND QUALITY-OF-LIFE ISSUES

Literacy impacts every aspect of our lives from infancy through adulthood. No one can question the importance of literacy for independent adult behavior. Rather, literacy skills are a critical component of an independent adult life. The lack of literacy is considered characteristic of school failure—a failure to learn (Kliewer & Landis, 1999).

Literacy acquisition can have a profound impact on quality-of-life indicators such as self-esteem, self-determination, independence, information gathering, the ability to learn, and enjoyment. Such quality-of-life indicators are equally important for students with significant disabilities as they are for individuals with no disabilities.

Self-Esteem

Being perceived as literate promotes a positive self-image. Being able to gather information from written material and create messages for others gives the impression of competence. Young children enjoy holding books and pretending to read long before they have mastered conventional reading skills. The same can be said for students with significant disabilities. Students seem to strive to imitate their more capable peers. For example, a student with severe and multiple disabilities, who was deaf, nonverbal, and used a wheelchair, liked to hold a pencil or pen and make marks on her papers in all of her general education high school classes. Her efforts to look like her peers were so important to her that she would resist the use of adapted materials (pictorial information) that would be more meaningful. Engaging in literacy activities connotes a level of maturity and positive feelings of self (Gordon Pershey & Gilbert, 2002). Supporting a student's development of self-esteem is one critical by-product of literacy learning.

Self-Determination

Learning to take charge of our lives and have control over critical factors is essential to most individuals. Children at a relatively early age strive for control by demanding preferred foods, toys, or activities and vehemently rejecting decisions made by their parents. Making choices and making those choices known to others are critical components of learning self-determination. Choices involving simple aspects of daily life, such as what to wear, toys to play with, and food to eat, serve as the foundation for learning how to make more complex choices, such as where to live, how to make a living, and whom to live with. The acts of reading, writing, and communicating interplay in the development of self-determination.

Unfortunately, students with severe disabilities, given their limited communication skills, have a difficult time making their preferences known (Turnbull & Turnbull, 2001). Individuals with significant disabilities may not know their options or even what options exist. They may be unable to obtain information from the written word and are dependent on others for information. In fact, in a national survey, Wehmeyer and Metzler (1995) revealed that individuals with mental retardation have very little control over their lives. Learning to recognize symbols (written text, pictures, objects) allows individuals to identify what is possible and then make decisions that indicate their preferences. Literacy skills that involve listening, communicating, reading, and writing are essential to the development of self-determination in individuals with significant disabilities.

Independence

The abilities to listen and comprehend, communicate effectively, read, and write allow a certain degree of independent performance that would not be possible without these skills. When language is understood (in whatever format), it is possible to act on the information provided (if it's within physical abilities). An overreliance on others to do things for you is avoided. For students with significant disabilities, one goal of education is to increase independence by teaching reading and understanding directions (e.g., pictorial, objects) to perform tasks (Agran, King-Sears, Wehmeyer, & Copeland, 2003; Copeland & Hughes, 2000). For example, being able to discern a restroom sign increases a student's potential for meeting personal needs without being directed by another person. Being able to recognize desired software or music CDs allows the student to obtain preferred activities and act on this preference without seeking assistance. Being able to follow pictorial/written directions to make Pizza Hut sauce at work avoids the need to be supported by a job coach or coworker. Independence via literacy is thus a goal for everyone, not just those with conventional literacy skills.

Information Gathering

One of the easiest and most convenient ways of gathering information is to read. Information is available in many different formats and assists us to get places, assemble items, order from a menu, obtain movie tickets, determine what's on TV, and numerous other tasks. Accessing information and giving information to others occur almost continuously throughout each day. Furthermore, individuals of all ages rely on available information portrayed in a number of ways in every environment. Young children may quickly recognize the signs advertising their favorite stores. They can read pictographic maps at the zoo and urge their parents to go to specific locations. They read cereal boxes and wrappers containing favorite foods and look for these same items when out shopping with their families. Young adults can peruse the newspaper to recognize a movie advertisement and make the request to go see the movie. Teaching all children to recognize the information that abounds in their environments and how to act on it are critical life skills that will aid them in their adult lives.

Organization

Literacy skills support an individual's ability to organize aspects of life. We use labels to file papers and put like items together. We write and read our daily schedules, take notes of things we need to do, and mark off those that are completed. We may alphabetize CDs, recipes, and file folders of important papers. We keep lists of phone numbers of family and friends close by to facilitate quick access to these people. All of these very practical examples of literacy use help make our lives easier and more manageable. Such organization skills also are of value to individuals having severe disabilities who need support to better understand their world and anticipate what is to come. For example, a student with significant disabilities may be able to accept a supported employment position at a music store and use the recognition of like symbols to place the same artist's work together. Numerous vocational positions depend on the ability to recognize similar symbols and organize accordingly.

Learning

Learning occurs through interactions with others. Learning occurs at any age, involves all subjects, and is lifelong. The impact of literacy on learning is obvious. Knowing how to read (whether in the conventional sense or not) opens the doors to every subject matter that is of interest. We learn from reading conventional text, accompanying pictures, and listening to others read. Through written expression, we can seek out additional information and receive feedback on what we have learned. The more efficient the literacy skills, the greater the opportunity to learn. Continued learning builds on what we have attained. For example, a 10-year-old boy with severe intellectual impairments, profound bilateral deafness, and myopia (nearsightedness) experienced snow during a hike in the mountains with his family. These experiences were captured in photographs and sent to school, where they were sequenced into a story with written text. Later in the year, when reading a story that involved snow and a snowman, this student grew excited, pointed repeatedly to the picture of the snow, then pointed up, put his head back, and spread his arms out, mimicking a reaction to snow falling on his face. He had learned the concept of "snow." All students have the same rights to learn and therefore the same right to literacy instruction.

Entertainment

Literacy allows us to read for pleasure, interact with others socially, and express ourselves in very creative ways. Literacy allows us to amuse ourselves alone and with others. We can share important aspects of ourselves with others who are important in our lives. We share experiences and build relationships. We can spend many hours reading books, doing crossword puzzles, sending e-mail messages, and accessing the Internet. We are amused by reading comic strips and joke books. We send greeting cards to friends and family, take photographs, and organize these artifacts in albums to preserve memories. The need to engage in meaningful leisure activities is important for all individuals and is particularly critical to those students who are limited in their abilities to physically explore and engage in certain activities. Having access to literacy materials enriches our lives by giving us pleasure.

WHY TEACH READING TO STUDENTS WITH SEVERE DISABILITIES?

Reading provides an autonomous means of obtaining information and gaining enjoyment. In addition, reading can facilitate social relationships as we discuss what we have read with one another. Each person reads for a variety of different reasons at different times. What is read is also individually determined. The reasons for reading are the same whether or not there is a significant disability present. Reading opens doors to the world and, as such, cannot be denied to those individuals whose complex disabilities will make learning to read a bit more challenging.

Recognizing its importance for *all* students, regardless of labels and real or perceived limitations, is essential for all teachers and families. Therefore finding ways to bypass barriers to learning (and teaching) literacy is imperative. Broadening the definition of literacy to include the building blocks of social experiences and different ways to represent these experiences (e.g., pictorial, object) makes it possible to include all students in learning literacy. In essence, as Katims (2001) asserts, teachers will need to define literacy individually for each student. In this way, we can ensure that no child is left behind.

2 Literacy and Communication

KEY CONCEPTS

- A close relationship exists between literacy and communication.
- Typical activities that involve social interaction and positive relationships facilitate children's acquisition of literacy skills.
- Adaptations and accommodations can be used to support a child's active involvement in literacy activities.
- Emergent literacy skills are important not only for young children, but for those of all ages.
- The use of augmentative communication devices strongly supports the development of literacy as messages are selected.
- Shared experiences can be drawn, photographed, or tactilely represented for literacy learning.

Communication and literacy are integrally related. Communication supplies the basic foundation for literacy learning and, as such, makes it possible for everyone to experience literacy (McSheehan, Sonnenmeier, & Jorgensen, 2002; Neuman, 1999). Anyone engaged in a communicative act is also engaged in the initial steps of literacy learning. The more sophisticated the communication, the greater ease there is in accessing literacy activities and benefiting from them. However, everyone communicates in some form or another, and therefore family members and professionals can take advantage of this fact and use communication as the bridge to literacy learning.

THE RELATIONSHIP BETWEEN COMMUNICATION AND LITERACY

Literacy learning begins at home as children naturally interact with their families (Adams, 1990; Anderson, Hiebert, Scott, & Wilkinson, 1985; Neuman, 1999). Children acquire language through observation and interaction with others, which lays the foundation for representational learning. The beginning steps for both communication and literacy consist of high-quality social interactions with another, which support the learning of basic concepts. People, actions, and things all have names or symbols, which can be heard, understood, written down and read. This essential relationship between communication and literacy is relevant whether or not a disability is present.

Typically developing children learn the names of people, items, and actions of interest and share this knowledge with family members using speech. Children talk about their experiences, dreams, and fears, and express their thoughts via drawing, scribbling, painting, and coloring. Children with significant disabilities who do not use speech will engage in alternative means of self-expression. They may use pictorial information, icons, and objects or parts of objects to make their needs and thoughts known. Although not as flexible or "all-encompassing" as speech, these alternative methods of communication can be very effective and can serve as a connecting bridge to the development of language and literacy.

BUILDING RELATIONSHIPS

One critical aspect of communication and, ultimately, literacy is the development of trusting relationships with others. Wanting to be with others and sharing experiences with them provide the basis for literacy learning. Very young children typically enjoy sitting close to a parent and listening to a story while they look at colorful pictures long before they can understand all of the spoken words and the full meaning of the story. Yet this fact does not deter family members from engaging in this important activity with the child. The physical and emotional closeness of this activity strengthens parental-child bonds. This activity of being read to becomes associated with positive parental attention while it develops an interest in the activity of reading.

Reading Together

Adults and older siblings can make the reading experience particularly enjoyable by making it fun, creating a positive atmosphere, using different noises and sound effects to increase interest, and adding humor. Initially, little may be expected of the child other than to be interested and enjoy the activity. Yet reading is not a passive activity for the child, but one in which increasing active involvement is the key. As the child develops, parents will point out certain pictures and colors and comment on these, further supporting the child's language skills (both receptive and expressive). To ensure the child's understanding of what is being read, parents will ask simple questions that become increasingly more complex and abstract as the child demonstrates his or her growing comprehension. Eventually, the parent will encourage the child to read with the parent pointing out words and then to read some of the words and phrases alone from memory. Rereading familiar stories supports the child's ability to do this and increases the child's confidence in his or her own reading skills (DeTemple, 2001; Hedberg & Westberg, 1993). Children will develop preferences for reading certain stories again and again, which helps them anticipate and predict what will happen and to recognize more aspects of the story in print or pictorial format. In general, reading with the parent highlights the importance of literacy for the child within a comforting and supportive environment.

The same benefits of reading to children without disabilities apply to those with disabilities even if they do not demonstrate the same succession of skills as their peers. The intimacy experienced during early reading with a parent or family member helps establish the trust needed for language development (Kliewer & Biklen, 2001). Children interact with those with whom they feel most comfortable. Joint attention to early reading and writing activities (e.g., being read to, looking at a photo album, making birthday cards) provides opportunities to interact and to become more aware of how literacy impacts simple daily routines.

Typically, the act of reading with a child is very interactive and much more a social event than just the narrow act of deciphering text. Children ask questions, point to favorite pictures, repeat spoken words, and add their own unique observations. Unfortunately, for children with complex disabilities with limited language abilities, this type of interaction is more difficult. They may not be physically able to point to a picture of interest. They may not have vision and so cannot see pictures or see the facial expressions of their parents. They may not be able to repeat words or noises or ask questions or even hear the story clearly. They may want a page reread but may not be able to make this wish clear. Parents may not have a clear idea of how their child is benefiting from the reading activity, and the child may be less reinforced for engaging in this critical activity as a result. Short attention spans and the inability to comprehend the story can interfere with typical reading activities.

However, the time spent together while reading and engaging in a variety of typical activities develops the trust and positive feelings that will

Table 2.1	Supporting the Child With Significant Disabilities in Literacy Activities

Considerations

- Has joint attention been established in the activity (either visually or tactilely)?
- Does the child have a way to interact? How?
- Is the child given many opportunities to reexperience the information?
- How will the activity be represented for communication/literacy purposes?
- Are highly responsive partners supporting the child's interest during the activity?

support these children in their future learning efforts. By engaging in activities with others and sharing experiences, whether or not they can understand everything about those experiences, children will learn a number of valuable skills. Caregivers may need to consider certain factors, such as how the child will respond and whether or not the child has had sufficient experiences to understand what is being read. Table 2.1 provides some aspects of literacy learning that may support the child's understanding. In addition, the adult reading the story might pick short stories or read only for a very limited time initially, gradually increasing the amount of time as the child shows an increased interest. The use of exaggerated facial expressions, interesting sound effects, and using rhythm or singing the words also might help increase the child's motivation to engage in reading time.

Fortunately, reading material that is commercially available to all children has become more interesting and interactive. Several products allow a child to touch a picture on a page and hear speech or sound effects that go with the story. LeapPad products are one such example and cover a relatively wide age range as well as ability levels. Even without supportive material, reading to children having significant disabilities can become an important familiar routine that is positive for both adult and child. For instance, one mother known to the author regularly read to her son, who had severe physical and cognitive disabilities, blindness, and deafness. Although she was not sure exactly what her son gained from the stories that were read, she knew that her son enjoyed these close times together.

The Benefits of Play Interactions

Researchers have investigated the effect of play, especially pretend play, on early literacy skills in preschool and kindergarten (Justice & Pullen, 2003; Katz, 2001). Children who engaged in pretend play activities with their parents showed a positive association with higher receptive vocabulary tasks and emergent literacy tasks in general (Katz, 2001). Play not only helps form positive relationships with others and increase social skills, but play that involves pretend talk aids in children's use of symbolic language. This, in turn, lays the foundation for early literacy learning.

Unfortunately, determining how children who have severe physical and sensory impairments will actively engage in play activities continues to challenge the field (Cress, 2003). These children may not benefit from hearing others use pretend play talk during play or from seeing the use of props, costumes, and the actions of others. Children with severe physical disabilities may not be able to handle play objects or to engage in active play with their parents, siblings, or peers. They become more passive observers of the playful interactions around them. Furthermore, without speech, they are limited in contributing to the use of language in play. Even with the addition of augmentative communication devices, they may be limited in their meaningful contributions by the symbols and messages that are on their devices. Children having severe cognitive impairments may be challenged by the highly abstract and symbolic nature of pretend or dramatic play. Adults and children trying to encourage play behavior may not receive the social reinforcement that they need to continue this effort.

Finding ways to increase the meaningful participation of children with the most significant disabilities in play activities is critical. These children need high-quality play opportunities to support the development of communication, understanding of symbolic language, and emergent literacy skills. Even if children cannot participate in the same manner as their peers without disabilities, they should still be provided with opportunities to experience all types of play, including pretend play. They can be given simple choices to make that will determine what pretend characters may do and that direct the play, which is physically manipulated by a peer without disabilities. They can be supported to dress up in costumes to better assume different pretend roles and have access to a variety of items, and be supported to use these items in play. They can be supported to play a role of a character as part of the dramatic play and provided with the appropriate speech-generating device (a voice output communication device), which will add to the play. Assistive technology in the form of simple switches and switch-operated toys can help bypass physical limitations and allow for a more active role in play. Some toys may fit easily into the play scenario, such as a switch-operated toy fire engine when pretending to be firemen, toy elephants operated by switches when playing "zoo," and switch-operated toy clowns when engaged in a circus theme. When other characters are needed as part of the play activity, it may be possible to make (or buy) puppets and place them over a switch-operated toy (e.g., a clown or robot toy). In this way, children can actively control important characters in a pretend play routine.

EMERGENT LITERACY FOR STUDENTS OF ALL AGES

Typically, early skills in literacy, such as recognizing that a book must be held a certain way, that pages are turned, that pages contain information in various forms that relate to different things, and that you can express yourself by writing (scribbling) on a page, are expected of or taught informally to quite young children during everyday interactions with adults (usually family members). These very basic and introductory skills related to learning about literacy are called *emergent literacy skills* and are felt to be the beginning steps to more advanced and traditional aspects of literacy learning (Locke & Butterfield, 1998; Sulzby & Teale, 1991).

Despite the fact that emergent literacy skills often are associated with very young children, they have substantial relevance for students of any age who have significant disabilities. For a number of reasons associated with their particular disabilities (severe cognitive impairments, limited physical or visual abilities) and sociocultural factors (limited expectation for literacy development), students with significant disabilities may not follow the typical progression of literacy skills development (Kliewer & Landis, 1999; Romski & Sevcik, 1996). As a result, they may never engage in certain skills or may be considerably older before they begin to show skills expected of much younger children. Motivation to acquire literacy skills also may play a role in how quickly this is attained. Nevertheless, age should not be a deterrent to beginning literacy instruction.

Helping students of all ages interact more effectively with others, typically through a variety of augmented means, will not only support communication skills development but also impact the development of literacy skills (Foley, 1993). The symbolic representation of ideas used to communicate with another person, which typifies augmentative communication devices, forms a bridge to understanding literacy.

AUGMENTATIVE AND ALTERNATIVE COMMUNICATION DEVICES

Augmentative and alternative communication devices (AACs) are, by their very nature, tools of literacy (Mirenda & Erickson, 2000; Romski & Sevcik, 1996). These devices can be either very low technology, such as drawn pictures on a board, or highly technological devices, such as a DynaVox, with a voice output and a dynamic screen similar to that of a computer, which allows the user to quickly access different communicative overlays for different social situations. Augmentative communication devices typically involve a visual or tactile display (e.g., picture or part of

Figure 2.1 Sample Overlay of an Eight-Message Augmentative Communication Device (Tech Talk), Which Shows the Relationship Between Stating a Message and Reading/Writing

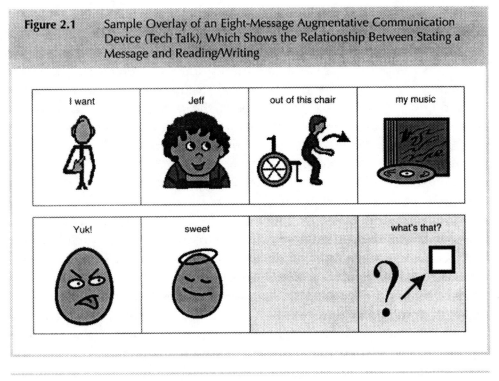

© The Picture Communication Symbols.

an object) with a written and/or voice output message. When the person using the device selects a message from the device, he or she is *reading* the available messages and *writing* the desired message. Although reading and writing may not be done in the conventional manner, the end result is the same. As Koppenhaver (2000) attests, "The use of augmentative communication devices is an integral part of literacy" (p. 270). You cannot use the device to communicate the message without engaging in literacy.

Teachers and family members can build on this basic relationship between augmentative and alternative communication devices and literacy by highlighting this aspect for the user. The print message should *always* be added to any symbol in a clear, bold, and easily readable font whether or not the student is presently reading the print. Figure 2.1 provides one such example. Repeating the message the student has indicated while pointing to the words will help draw the child's attention to the symbolic representation of the message, while modeling the desired behavior. The child learns that the symbols (e.g., print, pictures, or objects) on the augmentative device have meaning. The more opportunities that are provided to engage in communicative exchanges, the more experience the student receives in recognizing that symbols have meaning and convey information. Developing this concept of words can lead to sight word reading and more advanced literacy skills (Gately, 2004).

Although augmentative communication devices play a vital role in the development of both increased communication and literacy, they also can be limiting. Without considerable care taken to keep the device(s) changing and growing with the student's needs, the student may be restricted to only a few messages that he or she hears, sees, and reads and may become discouraged with the inability to communicate more fully. Furthermore, if augmentative communication devices have a limited number of messages and are used only in specific situations (e.g., to request food and drink at mealtimes), their use may not generalize to other environments and activities (Beukelman & Mirenda, 1998). Obviously, when engaged in literacy activities (being read to, being encouraged to draw), students need to have easy access to communication devices that allow them to ask questions, request more materials, comment on the story or drawing, and request more or an end to the activity. The use of augmentative and alternative forms of communication increases the student's active participation in literacy activities, making it more enjoyable and relevant. Those supporting the child will need to be aware of communication opportunities and expectations of various activities. Once aware of these types of learning opportunities, it will be up to those supportive team members to ensure that the child has the means to take advantage of such opportunities.

Although no one augmentative communication device will meet all communication needs, the availability in different situations is important. Children not using speech to communicate, or not using it effectively, need to be encouraged to use a wide array of augmentative and alternative communication throughout the day. Regular use helps strengthen communication as well as emergent literacy skills. AAC, whether homemade or commercial, should allow the student to make comments, request items or help, and ask questions during literacy-building experiences, such as interactive play, having a story read, drawing, or watching a video. While engaging in literacy-related activities is the first step, attention must also be paid to how the child is involved. Joint attention on relevant information (e.g., pictures, tactile items) is essential so that the child can connect what is heard to what is seen, felt, and physically engaged in. For children with significant disabilities, especially if a severe visual impairment is present, physically experiencing what others are seeing is very important. Instead of joint visual attention, mutual tactile attention is needed (Downing & Chen, 2003). In mutual tactile attention, the child's hands feel representative items as well as the hands of the conversation partner on the same item. In this way, the child realizes that their joint attention is on the same referent. Demands are not made of the child (e.g., the adult's hands are not used to physically prompt the child to perform a skill), but instead the hands of both individuals mutually feel what is being presented as a way of sharing the experience. The child can't see what the adult is looking at, but through touch can gain assurance that they are both engaged in the same activity.

BUILDING SHARED EXPERIENCES FOR LITERACY DEVELOPMENT

Sharing experiences with others provides the foundation for effective communication (Durand, Mapstone, & Youngblood, 1999). Since one form of communication is written, shared experiences are also critical for making literacy meaningful. We typically write about things that we know and have experienced, and we can easily associate with a writer when we have experienced similar things. For instance, reading about an adventure in another country can be understood, but it is even more meaningful if the reader also has been to that country. Of course, we can read about things that we have not experienced and gain information and enjoyment from the reading, but it is harder to picture and harder to relate than something that is shared between reader and writer.

Young children enjoy reading books about experiences they have had. They also enjoy the interaction that occurs as part of this literacy time. In fact, reading a story to a child is more than just the actual reading of the story; it also involves the interactions that naturally occur between the reader (usually an adult) and the child (Adams, 1990; Bloome & Katz, 1997; Koppenhaver, Erickson, & Skotko, 2001). The adult elaborates on the story by asking questions and relating it to the child's own experiences, thus making it more interesting and meaningful. The child is assisted to associate the written words and pictures with events in his or her life. The child learns that one way to share experiences is to document them in a story. A critical responsibility of early care providers is to ensure that children have numerous experiences during their developing years to promote comprehension of symbolically represented materials.

When children or adults struggle to understand pictorial information in stories, other approaches will be needed to document experiences in which they have participated. These alternative approaches will be described in the following pages. However, documentation of experiences relies on regularly occurring exposure to different experiences for all individuals regardless of age or ability level. While the individual with severe and multiple disabilities may not gain the same skills and knowledge from such experiences as same-age peers without disabilities, there is no way to determine the impact without at least the opportunity to participate. Furthermore, while initial experiences may not appear to be enjoyed by the individual, probably due to unfamiliarity or change in a routine, repeated exposure over time can have quite the opposite effect. Therefore repeated attempts to help the individual understand the event are needed before the individual can make an informed decision as to whether it's pleasurable and desired or not. For example, many individuals (with or without disabilities) may be reluctant to go dancing if they do not feel comfortable on the dance floor and do not feel that they will be very successful. However, repeated practice dancing and increased familiarity with the environment and others present can greatly enhance the enjoyment of such an activity. Obviously, every effort should be made to make the experience a positive and supported one (for everyone). Offering the individual with significant challenges as much choice-making control as possible throughout an activity, especially a new one, is one way to provide positive support. The important point to remember is that the shared experiences create memories that can be documented in some manner (writing) and referred to later (reading). Therefore as experiences occur, thought should be given to different ways to document them in support of later literacy skills development.

Documentation of Shared Experiences

For children and adults who can access print, braille, or the spoken word, documenting shared experiences is not that difficult. Experiences can be written, brailled, or audiotaped and made available for future reading. Obviously, children and adults can write or record their own experiences to develop writing skills. However, when conventional forms of literacy are not readily available due to significant cognitive and other disabilities, another format must be used. These formats could include drawings, photograph books, and tactile books.

Drawings

Some students may be able to draw their experiences so that they clearly represent the event. Other students may be able to draw some of these experiences with someone else filling in as needed. Still others will be able to understand (read) the drawings and follow the event in that matter. This alternative form of writing and recording shared experiences provides a solid building block for future, although more conventional, forms of literacy and should also be encouraged. Drawings of experiences, no matter how rough, make it possible to document experiences soon after they happen without having to find suitable pictorial information elsewhere. Drawings may be particularly beneficial for activities that are quite unique and for which it would be difficult to find suitable pictorial information. Drawings should be presented in a sequential manner and with explanatory text so that the story is clear to anyone accessing it. As much as possible, individuals with significant challenges should have control over accompanying text by indicating preference of options provided.

Photograph Books

With the increasingly simple-to-use technology for taking photographs of shared experiences so readily available, photographic information provides another very usable format for those unable to access conventional literacy modes. Typical photograph books provide an easy conversation tool for anyone to use. Photographs draw our attention—we want to understand what we are seeing. These may be taken of shared events with others and form a story of that experience. The use of photographs encouraged adolescents at risk for academic failure to discuss their lives and future goals and build strong bonds to their schools and teachers (Kroeger et al., 2004). Photographs facilitate the asking of questions: Who's that person? What are you doing there? What's that? They encourage the social turn-taking so basic to typical conversations.

When used with students who cannot access the conventional forms of literacy, photographs provide a very concrete reminder of experiences. They need to be presented in a sequential manner that facilitates the story line, and, of course, the written text needs to be added to each photograph so that others can have access to conventional text. With digital photography, teachers and family members can easily capture the experiences and not worry about taking a bad picture or not getting what was desired. Access to the digital pictures is much faster and easier than conventional photography and allows anyone with some basic hardware (e.g., computer, camera, and printer) to create photographic books.

Photographic information may provide more meaningful information to some students who struggle to understand more abstract representations. For example, in her sewing class in middle school, Aricelli uses a written/photographic sequence to help her determine consecutive steps in an activity. Aricelli is pictured in a few of the steps and points to herself and signs a modified "ME" sign to show her recognition of herself. For Aricelli, this represents a first step in understanding that the photographic symbols have referents. She sees the photograph and her name and uses sign to indicate her understanding that this stands for her in the sentence, "Aricelli goes to sewing class."

Tactile Books

Some students are not able to access pictorial information and will need another format. These students may be blind (or functionally blind) or simply not understand the representative value of pictorial information. Books containing tactile items that represent shared experiences make an accessible format for these students. Although somewhat bulkier than most conventional books, tactile books do not have to be large or heavy. Items felt during the course of the experience can be used to represent that experience for the student, with only a piece of the item used in the tactile book. For instance, the experience of riding a horse on the weekend could be tactilely represented for the student by a small piece of a horse blanket and/or some horsehair from the mane that the child felt while riding the horse. Of course, it would be important to point this out to the child during the activity if this piece were to be considered a representative item. The actual item (or part of an item) felt by the child has greater representational value than a miniature of the item (e.g., a small plastic horse). While visually there may be a connection, tactilely such a miniature has absolutely nothing to do with the event.

Unlike vision, the touch of sense provides information in relatively small pieces (what the hands can feel at one time), and the individual must synthesize the information into a whole (Downing & Chen, 2003). The individual will need time to explore the representational item and relate it to its referent. Consequently, tactile representations must be carefully selected based on their tactile information and not on their visual appearance. Furthermore, these tactile items need to be used on a regular basis with students as they learn to request desired items, seek information about something they find interesting, and make comments about these interests. Once they understand that these objects represent items, actions, and people, they can make use of them in more conventional literacy activities. More information is provided on the development of tactile books and other literacy material in Chapter 3 of this text.

SUMMARY

Chapter 2 has highlighted the close relationship between literacy and the development of communication skills. Events that all individuals experience create opportunities to interact and share information and enjoyment. Such activities can be specifically geared toward literacy learning, such as reading and being read to, or they can be any activity, such as going to a store, museum, or park. Representing these activities allows individuals with significant disabilities to refer to them through whatever means connects their communicative attempts to more conventional reading and writing.

The more individuals with significant disabilities are provided with ways to express their thoughts and feelings, the more they will be engaged in establishing basic literacy skills. Helping individuals with very significant disabilities to retell their social stories to others not only supports the development of critical communication skills but also provides a means for acquiring competencies in literacy.

FREQUENTLY ASKED QUESTIONS

1. My student has very limited responses in general. I'm not even sure about basic communication skills. How do I know he's getting anything out of reading activities?

When students are unable to clearly communicate their thoughts and feelings, teaching becomes extremely challenging. Assuming that the student can't get anything out of literacy activities leaves both teacher and student with limited options. Therefore the most positive and least dangerous approach would be to assume that the student is, in fact, gaining from the literacy activities, and to keep trying.

Very careful observation of the student and interviews with significant others may be helpful in identifying how the student indicates pleasure and displeasure with something. Everyone involved in supporting this student's education should be trained to recognize these communicative behaviors and act accordingly. If the student is enjoying being read to, he or she should indicate the desire for more of the story to be read when the reader has paused momentarily. This request for more to be read could be a slight smile, movement of the hand, turn of the head, vocalization, or anything that has been used in the past to indicate the desire for an activity to continue. When the student demonstrates this behavior, he or she should be shown how to request more of something using a simple voice output or speech-generating augmentative communication device if that is what the student appears to desire. Pairing what the student is currently doing with a clearer alternative should make it easier for everyone to respond to and so further support this student's understanding of the device use.

Another suggestion would be to read stories to the student that are relevant as possible and/or contain humor. Dr. Seuss books, for example, are enjoyable to a wide age range due in part to their amusing use of words, rhyme, and outrageous illustrations. Some students are more responsive to books with pop-outs or buttons to press for sound effects. Whatever type of books or reading material is used, make sure that the student is given a choice, and look for subtle indications that one story may be preferred. For example, relaxed body tone while reading a certain book may indicate the student's pleasurable response and enjoyment of the activity.

Never force a child (or adult) to engage in literacy activities. The goal is to help the individual understand the value of the activity. If the individual refuses the offer to engage in a literacy activity, acknowledge the individual's preference and offer an alternative. Return to the activity (or a similar one) at another time, offer a choice of materials to read or write with, and try again. What seemed negative to the child at one time may be perceived much more positively at another time with different materials and when lots of choices are offered concerning what to read (or write), where, and for how long.

2. How do I know which augmentative communication device is the best one for my student?

Determining the most appropriate alternative forms of communication other than speech for a student to use can be challenging. Fortunately, there is no need to identify the one "best" device. We all use multiple modes of communication, and each student who does not use speech as the primary mode of communication will make use of several alternatives during the course of each day (Beukelman & Mirenda, 1998; Cress, 2003; Downing, 2004).

Rather than focus on a specific type of communication, the emphasis can and should be on increasing the number and type of communicative exchanges throughout each day. Supporting the student's efforts to communicate during each daily routine and meaningful activity will help the student understand that things have names and that those names can be used to meet desires. Through any augmented communicated device, you make language visible or tactile and, by doing so, support the student's understanding of what it means to read and write (albeit in a less conventional manner).

Augmentative and alternative communication systems will reflect the needs and interests of the individual, the demands of the particular situation, and the social expectations of others. Some messages needed by the individual may extend across a number of critical environments and activities, such as, "I need a break" or "I want to say something else." Other messages may be needed only in specific situations, such as when requesting a certain flavored milk at lunch or asking a particular student to assist. In some environments, a voice output communication aid may help draw others to the person, while in others that are particularly noisy, the voice output may not be heard. In situations where the individual is working at a desk, the use of a somewhat bulky electronic device may work well, while at other times (e.g., playing at recess), a more portable and easy-to-handle system (or unaided system) is better. An unaided system would entail the use of facial expressions, gestures, manual signs, or anything that allows the student to communicate effectively without having to add anything (Beukelman & Mirenda, 1998). Encouraging the individual to engage in a number of different behaviors to express what is most relevant probably makes the most sense. Many individuals with complex communication needs prefer to use very-low-technological aids (e.g., an alphabet board) or rely on gestures and vocalizations when engaged in conversation with familiar partners (Cress & Marvin, 2003; Rowland & Schweigert, 1993). The idea is to use whatever helps the individual to be the most effective communicator, realizing that effectiveness of the communication exchange will differ depending on factors in the social environment.

3. What if my student has had very limited experiences and does not seem to understand what is being read?

This is a common challenge. Sometimes teachers know that their students have not experienced different activities, while other times it's not known. Obviously, the best solution is to support the student to experience as many different events as possible. Sometimes family members and friends are in a position to provide these experiences, and sometimes they are not. When experiences have been limited at home, then this becomes an important responsibility for the team at school. Taking related trips into the community to gain needed experiences is certainly one option. Of course, this should be done with the student's typical classroom, for all students to experience.

While reading stories or other material to the student, it will be helpful to make use of pictorial information, tactile artifacts, photographs, or drawings. Use these throughout the reading activity, and relate back to them. It may also help to engage in puppet play for younger students and to act out scenarios for all ages to help the student understand what the story represents. Classmates may be very helpful at enacting different scenes for the student who may not have experienced what is being read.

Careful determination of the "big ideas" intended in the activity may help narrow the focus somewhat to determine what would be most relevant to teach. Relating these big ideas to what the student has experienced is also important. For example, a sixth-grade class is reading a story about a horse race. One student in this class has severe and multiple disabilities and is learning to look at pictorial information and understand it. Pictures of horses are used (as well as pictures of people who are main figures in the story). Since this young lady has experienced horseback riding as a form of therapy for her physical disabilities, every effort is made to relate the picture of the horses to photographs of her riding and to teach her the association between the pictorial information and what she has previously experienced. Teaching her all of the intricacies of the story being read and of the development of the main characters and conflicts is not the focus for her learning.

3 Planning Literacy Activities

KEY CONCEPTS

- Literacy materials should be easily accessible to students with severe disabilities.
- General education classrooms offer plentiful literacy experiences for students with severe disabilities, as well as access to the core curriculum.
- Literacy goals are highly individualized for students with severe disabilities and require family input.
- Literacy instruction begins with a determination of a student's present performance, family expectations, and daily opportunities.
- A collaborative and integrative approach of service delivery is recommended to provide literacy instruction.
- Literacy materials should reflect the chronological age of the student, physical and sensory needs and abilities, cultural background and preferences, and interests.
- Technology exists to support the literacy needs of students with severe disabilities.

Since students with severe and multiple disabilities may not be accessing literacy activities in the same manner as other students, some thought must go into planning. The typical array of literacy materials and experiences may need to be adapted, at times significantly, to allow a given student access. How this will occur and expected outcomes for the student need to be clearly stated and understood by all members of the team. This chapter will address some of the main issues when planning for literacy activities that will include everyone.

GENERAL CONSIDERATIONS

Research in literacy for students in general advocates for several components to be in place. The environment must be supportive of literacy, both the social as well as physical environments (Fisher & Kennedy, 2001). Teachers must be trained to consider this critical skill in all of their activities with students. They must be skilled in a variety of teaching techniques to address the diverse needs of students in their classes. Several different strategies can be employed to teach literacy, which means that the teachers must not only be knowledgeable about these strategies, but must know how to implement them and to what degree (and in what combination) to be effective with all students. Even when disabilities are not considered, each classroom usually contains a widely diverse group of learners who respond quite differently to different teaching strategies. With increased emphasis on accountability from No Child Left Behind legislation, teachers find themselves under considerable pressure to raise literacy scores for all students. Fortunately, recommended practices for enhanced literacy learning in general also apply to students with significant impairments, especially the provision of literacy-rich environments.

Literacy-Rich Environments

Classrooms considered supportive of literacy activities are filled with printed information, often supported with colorful pictures that attract attention (Allington & Baker, 1999; Fisher & Kennedy, 2001). Everywhere students look, the power of the written word is apparent. Rooms are decorated with word walls, poems, the daily schedule, and class rules. Students can quickly see how words provide information on a variety of topics. Their own written work is displayed, which further strengthens and personalizes the importance of writing and reading. In younger grades, the alphabet may be posted on the wall or at each desk. Posters of classic novels and those with catchy sayings appear on rooms in secondary classrooms.

While print is readily available to students who have vision and can understand the meaning of the printed word, students with severe and multiple disabilities who may not have vision and/or may not have a basic understanding of print are at a distinct disadvantage. Pictorial information paired with the written words can create an awareness of literacy for those who do have vision. Therefore pictorial information displayed around the classroom should play a vital role in making literacy accessible. For students who need to obtain information via the tactile sense, consideration must be given to decorating the room with interesting tactile information as well as pictorial and print. While perhaps easier to do in preschool and elementary classrooms, adding pictorial and tactile information to any classroom at any age is certainly feasible. Students without disabilities can offer suggestions to make this a possibility and can help in the design of the room. Tactile objects and parts of objects can extend off of bulletin boards and walls, along with pictorial and written material. The student needing this type of adapted material will need to be encouraged to explore the classroom environment to be made aware of what is present. Time must be allowed for such exploration, since the student will not be able to access it quickly or at a distance as other students are able to do. For example, a sixth-grade class was studying China during social studies. In addition to posters and other pictorial information on the walls and bulletin boards, silk scarves representing this Chinese product as well as pairs of chopsticks, a Chinese parasol, and a colorful paper Chinese dragon had been added to one bulletin board for all students to enjoy, but specifically for the student who is blind and has severe and multiple impairments.

In preschool and elementary classrooms, reading areas can be designated where students can easily access self-selected reading material whenever they have finished their work. Reading areas can be decorated with posters encouraging reading and contain comfortable beanbag chairs, large pillows on a carpet, or even a small sofa. In addition to a variety of high-quality reading material (books, magazines) that represent a relatively wide range of reading levels, a tape recorder or CD player with headphones should also be present with choices of reading material on tape or CD. Students should also be encouraged to read to one another, sharing books, which is particularly supportive of students unable to access conventional print. The ultimate goal of such a reading area is to make it welcoming and inviting to all children, so that reading is perceived as a relaxing and entertaining pursuit. This area also should be accessible to a student using a wheelchair and/or should have adaptable positioning equipment for students unable to sit unsupported.

Beyond classroom walls, students of all ages should be encouraged to frequently visit the school library. Students will need instruction on how to find certain kinds of books, where magazines are kept, and how to use computer technology to find desired information. Selecting and checking out books are specific skills that are helpful for all individuals at various times in their lives. Students with severe and multiple disabilities are not precluded from such instruction, but will be taught how to make choices of books, reading material, and tapes; how to check out books; and how to request assistance as needed. A special section of the library can house tactile books that contain textures, objects, and parts of objects that tell a story for those students unable to see or understand pictures. These books can be made by the family, teachers, volunteers, and/or by the student with help from peers or adults.

Skills acquired in a school library can transfer to a public library in the student's community if students are encouraged to frequent these as well. Family members can support school efforts at literacy learning by helping their children acquire library cards and encouraging them to go to the library on a regular basis. Students with severe and multiple disabilities also need this kind of support to access a public library and benefit from that experience.

BENEFITS OF LEARNING IN A GENERAL EDUCATION CLASSROOM

Considerable research exists to support the learning of students with severe disabilities in general education classrooms (Fisher & Meyer, 2002; Fisher & Ryndak, 2001; Hunt & Goetz, 1997; Ryndak & Fisher, 2003). Benefits for students with and without disabilities have been noted in a variety of areas, including communication, academics, social skills, behavior, and acceptance of diversity (Downing, Eichinger, & Williams, 1997; Fisher & Meyer, 2002; Freeman & Alkin, 2000; Logan & Malone, 1998). In the area of literacy, researchers have identified specific positive outcomes that support the inclusion of students with severe disabilities learning with their peers who do not have disabilities (Ryndak, Morrison, & Sommerstein, 1999). Students with significant disabilities can benefit from their peers' abilities to engage meaningfully in literacy activities. Classmates with no disabilities provide competent role models who speak, read, and write fluently (Davern, Schnorr, & Black, 2003). Students with significant disabilities see their peers handling papers, books, and pens and reading silently and aloud. They see classmates writing and typing on computers. The active engagement of peers can help students with significant disabilities gain greater interest in reading and writing activities and working with similar materials.

In general, typical classrooms offer a more stimulating environment with a wide range of activities for participation. While literacy instruction can occur in any environment, classrooms having many students who are independently engaged in the reading and writing process can provide the necessary additional support for students with significant disabilities to become involved in these same literacy activities. Opportunities for literacy instruction abound in general education classrooms where there are numerous and stimulating literacy materials available. Expectations for students to be engaged in literacy activities impact students with significant disabilities who are in these classes. When students with similar severe and multiple disabilities are placed together in a classroom, it becomes much more difficult for the teacher to maintain high literacy expectations. Other aspects of the students' disabilities may take precedence, such as health care and positioning, leaving less time for instruction in literacy that may be perceived as less important. As Kliewer and Landis (1999) warn, "When children were surrounded by presumed nonliterate classmates, they too struggled to be seen as literate and worthy of consistent, identifiable literacy experiences" (p. 98). On the other hand, when surrounded by literate classmates, students with significant disabilities also are expected to demonstrate literacy skills. They are provided with similar materials and are expected to use these materials for learning and demonstrating that learning.

Access to the Core Curriculum

A major benefit of educating students with severe disabilities in general education classrooms is the clear access to the core curriculum that is taught by an instructor who has had considerable training and experience with the core. Whereas general educators typically are trained in reading, writing, and literature, special educators, especially those working with students who have severe disabilities, receive much less training in these areas. It is much easier to ensure that students have access to multiple literacy activities throughout the day when these students are learning within typical classrooms. The expectation in general education classrooms is that students will be reading and writing and engaging in the written word across subject matter. With this expectation readily apparent, more effort may be made to also expect literacy behavior of students who cannot easily access typical literacy materials.

Core standards in literacy have been identified by each state in the nation. As much as possible, students with significant disabilities should be considered accountable for these standards to ensure that they are receiving quality instruction (Boundy, 2000). However, these core standards will need to be interpreted somewhat differently for students unable to show proficiency in the same manner as other students. For example, if a standard calls for students to demonstrate their ability to read to obtain information, the student with significant disabilities will be expected to reach this standard, albeit in a modified manner. This student may be expected to read a pictorial/written schedule to determine the next activity of the day. Or the student may be expected to read a tactile/written sequence of steps to determine the next step in an activity. Planning how each content standard will be interpreted for a given student with significant disabilities is necessary for effective instruction. Of critical importance is that students with significant disabilities have meaningful access to core standards and that there is an expectation for these students to show acquisition of these standards as they have been individually interpreted for the student. More information on the role of standards in measuring student progress is presented in Chapter 5 of this text.

Not Just Physical Presence

The goal of inclusive education is not physical integration (Downing, 2002; Fossett, Smith, & Mirenda, 2003; Kliewer, 1998). Rather, the goal of inclusive education is to ensure that all students are learning and are being challenged to learn to their maximum potential. Having exposure to literacy is a necessary premise, but is not the end goal. All students have a right to acquire as much of this valuable skill as possible. Therefore while physical placement of a student in a general education classroom may ensure a minimal level of exposure to literacy materials and activities, specific instruction in literacy goals and objectives is essential.

Students with significant disabilities should not just be passive recipients of literacy activities, such as when they are read to or shown pictures or drawings made by other students. They need to be actively involved in the learning process and supported to demonstrate what they know. Educators must assume the responsibility to identify specific skills that will most benefit the student and then undertake to teach these skills in the most relevant and efficacious manner. Such high-quality instruction should occur regardless of students' age, so that every student has as much access to literacy instruction during the school years as possible.

IDENTIFYING LITERACY GOALS

Every student is unique, and therefore what that student needs to learn in the area of literacy will be highly individualized. Students with severe disabilities do not necessarily follow a developmental model of concept mastery (Katims, 2001; Kliewer & Biklen, 2001; Kliewer & Landis, 1999). They may learn certain skills in a very unique manner depending on interests, experiences, abilities, and expectations of others. They may never be able to acquire what might be considered very basic skills, such as producing the sounds of letters, because they do not have the physical control to do so. Identifying individual literacy goals for each student is a critical first step in appropriate planning.

Students with severe and multiple disabilities may fail to see the purpose of standardized assessment tools and often do not possess the skills necessary to perform well on such assessments. Such instruments have been criticized for inappropriate use with students who have significant disabilities (Browder & Spooner, 2003; Erickson & Koppenhaver, 1998). The information obtained from such an assessment may not provide the teacher (or family member) with practical information that can be used in implementing an effective intervention. For example, a student may not be able to perform very basic skills of reading due to blindness and a severe cognitive disability. Results on a standardized type of assessment may indicate that the student cannot progress beyond a literacy level of being read to, which, if taken seriously, could unduly restrict educational opportunities. Each student will have unique experiences and unique ways of demonstrating competence, and therefore measurement using a standardized format will not capture unique needs. An alternative approach is needed.

What Are the Literacy Goals of the Individual and the Family?

Since there can be many ways of teaching literacy skills, determining goals and expectations of the individual, when possible, and of the family is important. Do family members want the child to be able to entertain herself by looking at pictures in magazines and other such materials? Do they want their child to be able to write his name on important documents? Do they want their child to make use of some written information to avoid dangers? Do they want the child to sit quietly in church, holding a hymnal and turning the pages while the congregation sings? Do they expect their child to read on a certain grade level? Finding out from family members what literacy means to them and what their dreams are for their family member with a significant disability is critical information needed to guide the intervention process. While dreams may exceed actual accomplishments, learning about the dreams that families have for their children is a necessary start. For instance, one family often spent time reading together in the evenings. The parents both wanted their son, who had severe intellectual impairments, to be a part of this family activity. However, their son, at 19, had very limited literacy skills, did not read in the traditional sense of the word, and often interrupted this family activity. Teaching this young man to select appropriate reading material, hold the material properly, attend to the pictorial information, turn the pages, and when possible, listen to an audiotaped recording of the material would help include this young man in a familiar family activity. Being aware of such a goal can help guide the educational team when considering literacy activities.

This person-centered approach to identifying literacy goals is an important first step to additional assessment (Browder, Fallin, Davis, & Karvonen, 2003). Instead of assessing the student according to the literacy skills expected of others the same age, the student is assessed according to desired goals and expectations of the student (when possible) and the family or significant others. For example, if the family wants their child to be able to sign his name by using a signature stamp appropriately, then the student's ability to perform this skill when needed is assessed. The skills typically considered as prerequisite for writing one's name (e.g., letter recognition, letter naming, writing individual letters) are not assessed. The main objective of this type of assessment procedure is not to identify deficit skill areas, but to help the team determine what is important to teach as well as effective ways to teach it. Such an approach is highly individualized and takes into account cultural, familial, and religious preferences.

In addition to familial input in determining literacy goals, state standards in literacy also should be included (Kleinert, Haigh, Kearns, & Kennedy, 2001; Thompson, Quenemoen, Thurlow, & Ysseldyke, 2001). Every state has academic standards that each student at different grade levels is supposed to master. Interpreting these standards so that they are meaningful to an individual student, while also maintaining the individualization required by a student's individualized education plan (IEP) requires a somewhat delicate balancing act for the educational team. Both requirements are important in determining appropriate literacy goals. For example, a standard for 11th grade might target the development of a creative story, while parents may desire their child to express herself more effectively. An IEP goal that addresses the student's ability to create a story about herself by sequencing photographs in order would meet both the standard and the family's preference.

Determining Present Literacy Skills

Of obvious importance is the need to determine what students with significant disabilities are presently doing with regard to literacy, especially as they relate to desired goals. While not advocating a developmental approach to literacy skills mastery, it is helpful to know what skills are present so as to build on those skills, determine means of using them in different situations and environments (generalization), and identify skills that are needed but are lacking. Physical abilities, the presence or lack of vision and hearing, communicative competence, experiences, and motivation will all play roles in literacy skills demonstration and mastery. For instance, a student may know that a book needs to be righted and oriented in a different way but may not be able to perform this particular skill because she can't control her hands or limbs well. However, if this same student can communicate to a partner, by squealing or giggling, that the book is upside down or angled incorrectly, the student should be given credit for recognizing how a book needs to be held to be read. A student who is deaf and has additional disabilities may not be able to say the name of the letter, but may point to a letter on a page that is the same first letter of his name and point to himself, indicating that he recognized this letter. Another student may recognize when a partner has finished reading a page and will tap on the page to indicate the need to read the next page. This student is indicating that he knows that something has been mapped onto the paper and that it has meaning. He should be given credit for this understanding. Assessing students' performance as they naturally engage in a variety of different activities will provide a more accurate indicator of what the student can do than assessing students in a formal and out-of-context testing situation.

With regard to writing skills, documenting what the student can do versus taking a deficit approach is recommended. Developmentally, the student may be several years behind others his or her age, yet the focus should be on what skills the student is currently demonstrating and where those skills may lead. For example, a student may not be able to write any letters, but may be able to grasp a writing implement with an adapted gripper and make marks on paper. This skill demonstrates the student's understanding of a basic step in writing and perhaps the motivation to write. When developing the present level of performance for this student, stating what the student does within the realm of writing versus saying that the student does not write is limiting and does not provide practical information for the teacher. Other examples of demonstrated "writing" skills may include using a signature stamp to sign one's name, recognizing that there is a special place to put one's name, tallying the score at a game, sequencing photographs to tell a story from home, placing a mark on the picture that goes with the spoken or signed word, or activating a switch to select a pictorial symbol to be used on a report. While perhaps not conventional writing skills, they do indicate what the student knows about written expression, and they do provide a starting point for teaching more conventional skills.

Analyzing the Environment and the Need for Literacy Skills

When it is obvious that the student may not be able to gain all essential and perhaps conventional literacy skills, the focus should be on what literacy skills will be the most practical and enjoyable for the student across a number of different activities and environments. Instead of focusing on all the skills that a same-age peer might learn, greater attention may need to be paid to the types of literacy skills that will most benefit the student—those that occur with the greatest frequency. For instance, if the family enjoys eating out a lot, teaching the student to read a pictorial menu may be a very practical skill for that student. The same skill may be much less meaningful for a student who rarely, if ever, eats out. As another example, helping a student read CD music labels to find favorite CDs may be very meaningful for one student who loves music, and have much less meaning for students uninterested in playing CDs. Obviously, family lifestyles, culture, religious beliefs, and aspirations will help guide the educational team in identifying the most critical literacy skills to be targeted for any given student.

Analyzing the student's daily environment at home and in the general education classroom will help identify frequently needed literacy skills for the student. Two such ecological inventories of literacy skills are identified in Table 3.1 for a second grader and Table 3.2 for a tenth grader. While the students at both grade levels may not be able to read on grade level and therefore perform all skills as classmates without disabilities, knowing when these skills occur and what is involved will help identify when adaptations are needed. For example, when students can't access text easily, information in the texts will need to be adapted using pictures to help the students understand basic concepts and big ideas. Adaptations can be suggested next to each identified literacy skill, as in Tables 3.1 and 3.2. Initial suggestions to be used as adaptations may change once intervention has begun.

IDENTIFYING WHEN LITERACY SKILLS CAN BE TAUGHT THROUGHOUT THE DAY

Considerable literacy occurs naturally during each school day in general education settings. As a result, identifying when the student with significant disabilities will be instructed in literacy should not be a problem. However, since the student is probably not accessing material or creating written products in a similar fashion as peers without disabilities, determining how to meet their unique literacy needs across the school day will take some planning.

An IEP/activity matrix is recommended as a means of identifying when a given student's unique literacy needs can be addressed during the school day. Using this format, activities of the day are written across the top of the matrix, and the targeted skills, in this case literacy skills, are listed in the first vertical column. In the resulting boxes under each activity of the day, the team can determine how each skill will be addressed. Table 3.3 provides an example of such an activity matrix for a student in grade seven.

Table 3.1   Ecological Inventory of Literacy Skills

Student: Second grader with severe autism, nonverbal

Subjects	Literacy Skills	Adaptations Needed

Language Arts	Reading name to find folder
	Reading core literature
	Listening to others read
	Writing workshop
	
	Reading self-selected material
	  when work is completed
	Signing name on papers
		Highlight name
		Provide simple story and
		  pictorial information
		Use pictures and numbers
		  to sequence story line
		Offer 3 choices of
		  reading material
		Choose from 3 prewritten
		  names on sticky labels

Math	Reading name on math folder
	  and materials
	Listening to instructions
	
	Reading instructions on board
	
	Writing word problems
	Signing name on paper
		Highlight name
		
		Use manipulatives to
		  demonstrate very
		  simplified math task
		Use stickers to write with
		  and create equations.
		Use number stamps
		Choose from 3 prewritten
		  names on sticky labels

Social Studies	Reading name on social
	  studies text
	Reading chapter text
	
	Listening to others read
	Reading questions at end of
	  chapter
	
	Writing answers to questions
	
	Writing name on answer sheet
		Highlight name
		
		Add pictures to ones in text
		  and draw attention to these
		  pictures as text is read
		Let student choose reader
		Simplify questions and use
		  Writing with Symbols
		  2000 to represent
		Use pictures to answer
		  from choice of 3
		Choose from 3 prewritten
		  sticky labels

Lunch	Reading name on lunch ticket
	
	Reading magazines after eating
	
	Listening to peers read notes
		Highlight name, have some
		  space around student's card
		Use magazines with many
		  pictures, offer a choice
		Ask peers to act out some of
		  what they are reading

Art	Reading name on art work
	Reading instructions on
	  blackboard
	Listening to teacher instructions
	Signing name on art work
		Highlight first letter on name
		Use pictorial/written text of
		  instructions
		
		Use Post-it labels to sign

Table 3.2   Ecological Inventory of Literacy Skills

Student: Tenth grader with Rett syndrome and severe intellectual disability

Subjects	Literacy Skills	Adaptations Needed
Ceramics	Reading name on projects	Use colored Post-its
	Reading directions	Use pictorial/written simplified directions
	Reading labels on materials	Add pictorial/written label to cupboards
	Reading daily planners	Use pictorial/written planner
Driver's Ed	Reading driver's education book	Simplify text with most meaningful pictures/words
	Reading worksheets	Simplify and use pictures/words on worksheets
	Signing name to worksheets	Use labels, highlight correct name
	Taking tests	Simplify and use pictures of most relevant information
	Reading daily planner	Use pictorial/written planner
Earth Science	Reading text	Simplify and add pictures for most important relevant information
	Reading worksheets	Simplify and use pictures to read and write with
	Reading/writing instruction from board	Provide simplified pictorial sequence of steps
	Signing names to worksheets	Use labels to choose from, highlight correct name
	Taking tests	Simplify and use pictures to read and take test
	Reading daily planner	Use pictorial/written planner
Photography	Reading name on work folder	Highlight name
	Reading labels on cupboards for materials	Add pictures to labels
	Reading directions of how to take pictures and develop film	Photographic sequence of steps
	Taking adapted tests	Simplify and use pictorial information
	Reading daily planner	Use pictorial/written planner
Consumer Math	Reading name on work folder	Highlight name
	Reading text	Simplify and use pictures with few words
	Reading worksheets	Simplify and use pictures/words
	Signing name to worksheets	Use labels, highlight correct name
	Reading/writing directions from board	Provide simplified pictorial sequence of steps
	Reading daily planner	Use pictorial/written planner

Table 3.3   IEP/Activity Matrix Literacy Skills of a Seventh Grader

Skills	Language Arts	Earth Science	Social Studies	Lunch	Math	PE
Identify his name from 3 options	When signing papers to be turned in	When signing papers to be turned in	When signing papers to be turned in	When identifying his lunch ticket	When signing papers to be turned in	When identifying his workout sheet from others
Make controlled vertical marks on paper	Writing the number 1 when answering questions, tallying characters in stories	Tallying during science projects, marking off steps completed	Writing the number 1 when answering questions, marking spots on maps	Keeping scores for games when played	When tallying for probability, counting, representing numbers	Tallying laps run, checking off weight-lifting stations
Read symbols for activities of the day	Read daily planner at beginning of each period	Read daily planner at beginning of each period	Read daily planner at beginning of each period	Read daily planner at beginning of each period	Read daily planner at beginning of each period	Read daily planner at beginning of each period
Answer comprehension questions using pictures	After reading literature in class	After every topic discussed in class	After every story or topic discussed in class or researched on Internet		When relating math problems to real-life situations	For tests on physical conditioning, when asked about appropriate equipment to use
Stamp name on designated line	When signing his name on papers or projects	When signing his name on papers or projects	When signing his name on papers or projects		When signing his name on papers or projects	When signing his name on workout routine

Different learning opportunities will exist for students depending on their age, grade, and learning environment. Since literacy involves basic skills that are essential to learning all subject matter, it is not difficult to identify literacy opportunities as they naturally occur throughout each day. The main difficulty may be that the reading and writing levels may be considerably more advanced than the student with severe and multiple disabilities is able to comprehend. Information will need to be adapted for these students and expectations adjusted so that they can be successful. The focus is on how to effectively include the student, not exclude him or her based on perceived deficits.

Creating Literacy-Learning Opportunities for All Ages

Although conventional literacy activities are clearly present in general education classrooms, not all students will be able to benefit from these activities without considerable support. To provide more practical and continuous opportunities to engage in meaningful literacy activities, adjusting expectations and modifying the activity will be needed. For instance, instead of relying only on auditory information to follow directions in a class, those directions can be pictorially depicted, with simple phrases listed to provide the opportunity to read the directions. Students can learn to recognize color words written in their respective colors during an art class or when being introduced to any concept that involves color (e.g., the colors green and brown during a topic on plants in an earth science class).

While prospects of literacy skills acquisition may appear more promising during the primary years, there is no reason to be pessimistic as the student ages. Students with the most complex disabilities, including a severe to profound intellectual impairment, may take longer to understand how events in their lives are represented. It may not be until middle or high school years that they begin to understand that events can be recorded on paper or computer. The challenge will be to support early literacy learning using materials that do not reflect negatively (in a too-juvenile manner) on these older students. Creating age-appropriate means of addressing literacy skills that the student can practice throughout each day will be critical. The IEP/activity matrix approach described previously can help alleviate this concern, as well as seeking input from all team members.

Integrated Related Services

Learning literacy is of critical importance and should be the concern of all educational team members regardless of their specialized roles. Furthermore, literacy occurs everywhere, and so everyone on the team needs to be able to make use of available learning opportunities. For instance, the Orientation and Mobility Specialist working with a student on more independent travel from the classroom to the restroom will want to ensure that the student feels the raised icon and the braille words on the restroom door before entering. The Adapted Physical Educator working with this same young man will want to help him find his locker by searching for the tactile marker that has been added and the braille name that is right next to it. The student's PE clothes are labeled with a braille marker, and so this teacher will help him feel for his name before changing his clothes. Although the focus of these instructors' service is not to teach literacy, they can support the efforts of the team as they encounter opportunities to read and write during their instructional time with the student.

Recommended practices in the field advocate an integrative service delivery model in which each specialist on the team incorporates his or her expertise and knowledge into the typical classroom and meaningful routines of the day (Craig, Haggart, & Hull, 1999; Downing, 2002; Hunt, Soto, Maier, & Doering, 2003). Such a service delivery model is highly collaborative with various members of the team engaging in role release and sharing of information to most effectively meet the needs of the student. Instead of removing a student from a class to engage in isolated therapy services, the specialist enters the classroom and works in coordination with the teacher, paraprofessional, and other members of the team to support the development of critical skills when and where they are needed. Each member of the team must not only be knowledgeable with regard to his or her own area of expertise but also have a general knowledge of the entire program for the student and critical goals to which the student aspires. For example, the speech and language pathologist not only targets basic communication needs but also is aware of physical considerations, visual needs and limitations, and effective teaching strategies. Structuring the time to meet and share information and ideas is critical for a true collaborative approach (Downing, Spencer, & Cavallaro, 2004; Hunt et al., 2003). Finding the time to meet as a team may be one of the most challenging aspects of collaborative teaming (Keefe, Moore, & Duff, 2004). While supporting literacy skills development is certainly related to the areas of expertise represented by service providers such as speech and language pathologists, teachers in the area of vision and hearing, and occupational therapists, it is also of concern for the physical therapist, adaptive physical educator, and behavioral specialist. Each service provider must be aware of the student's total program so that opportunities to engage in literacy learning can be utilized as they occur. When each adult in the student's life directs the student's attention to reading and writing opportunities, the message sent to the student is that this is important and something valued by everyone.

Since positioning is an important aspect of learning in general for students with severe physical disabilities, both the occupational therapist and the physical therapist can provide critical information in this area. They can recommend specific positioning equipment to support the acquisition of literacy skills, while also ensuring that the student is not isolated from other students. The occupational therapist in particular can recommend adapted writing tools, grips, slant boards, and page turners to ease the physical process of writing and reading. In addition to adaptive aids to use, the occupational therapist can recommend specific strategies to assist the student make the most controlled and efficient movements to aid in writing. The speech and language pathologist's role is intricately related to the development of literacy. Helping the student improve communication skills, through the use of augmentative and alternative communication, forms the basis for literacy learning. The speech and language pathologist can assist in the development of different overlays for the student to read, select, and share with others. How communication devices are selected and developed can have a major impact in helping the student recognize how common experiences, requests, and so on can be symbolically represented (written).

Often the student with significant disabilities will have direct support of a full-time paraprofessional in an inclusive setting. While an essential team member, the paraprofessional should not become the sole instructor for the student with the most complex disabilities (French, 2003; Giangreco, Edelman, Luiselli, & MacFarland, 1997). The special educator will provide direct instruction at times, while the paraprofessional supports other children in the class or other students with special needs in other classes. The special educator will have a caseload of students to prepare for with various general educators, adapt materials, teach, and monitor progress. This highly qualified professional will assume responsibility to train paraprofessionals who will support individual students with significant disabilities in different grades and classes as the need dictates. Any paraprofessional working in a general education classroom is under the direction of the general educator as well as the special education teacher, who will rotate among different classes. For more information on this type of teamwork, see Downing (2002) for examples at the preschool, elementary, middle, and high school levels.

While some members of the educational team have roles that bear directly on literacy learning (e.g., special educator, general educator, paraprofessional, occupational therapist), all members have the responsibility to support the acquisition of this valuable skill. A collaborative working relationship, in which all team members share their knowledge and expertise and readily assume (at least in part) the roles of other team members, helps create a unified educational program. Fragmented learning is avoided, and the student is assured greater consistency in instruction across many different activities and environments (Giangreco, Edelman, Luiselli, & MacFarland, 1996).

DEVELOPING LITERACY MATERIALS FOR INDIVIDUAL STUDENTS

A combination of handmade as well as commercially produced literacy materials will be needed to meet the literacy needs of students with significant disabilities. Whenever possible, making use of available materials used by all students is recommended. High-quality reading materials are available at all grade levels and in a variety of formats (e.g., print, audiotapes, CDs, DVDs, videos, filmstrips). When typical literacy materials are not accessible to students for cognitive, visual, or auditory reasons, then materials will have to be developed. The advantage of handmade materials is that they can be carefully tailored to the unique needs of the student and the activity. The disadvantage, of course, is that time is required to prepare the materials and have them ready. Although initially time-consuming, once the materials have been made, copies can be made and saved for future students. Schools and school districts can share adapted material to be as efficient as possible. Table 3.4 provides a list of strategies for educational personnel to use when consumables (pictures, objects, parts of objects) need to be obtained for different students.

Whether materials are handmade or commercially attained, they should reflect the following recommended characteristics of being age appropriate, interesting, and of high quality, as well as meeting individualized needs (Allington & Baker, 1999; Gambrell & Mazzoni, 1999). Of critical importance is the need to ensure that print (and, when needed, braille) is on *all* materials. Whether or not a student's reading skills are at a level of letter or word recognition, not having the traditional orthographic or braille information prevents any possibility of acquiring these skills. Accessibility demands that print (and braille) always accompany other, less symbolic means of reading (e.g., pictures, parts of objects). Furthermore, these traditionally written messages provide necessary information to communication partners interacting with the student. Figure 3.1 depicts an example of an adapted spelling test for a student who is learning to read pictures. As can be seen in this example, all pictures are labeled, whether or not the student has acquired this more conventional skill.

Table 3.4 Gathering Pictorial and Tactile Materials for Literacy Activities

- Develop ongoing lists of what is needed and make available in school's attendance office.
- Ask team members to help collect materials.
- Use fliers and school newsletters to ask families for assistance.
- Ask student teachers and early fieldwork practicum students to help with materials.
- Make requests for materials at parent-teacher organization meetings.
- Request community support—ask volunteer organizations like the Girl Scouts, Boy Scouts, Rotary clubs, religious groups.
- Establish a convenient drop-off site for materials.
- Access Web sites for free graphics on the Internet.

Figure 3.1   Sample of Adapted Spelling Test

© The Picture Communication Symbols.

Age Appropriateness

As much as possible, materials need to be chronologically age appropriate for students. As students age, they should experience different materials that reflect this growth and development. Otherwise, students will not have the opportunity to learn about different things and may become overly dependent on material that is considerably younger than they are. For example, a teenager may have become very familiar and comfortable with a story about Barney, the purple dinosaur, and insist upon the reading of this story, rejecting other options. This association with overly juvenile material may reduce expectations by others as well as reduce self-esteem. In addition, interacting with overly juvenile material may serve as a barrier to interactions with others of the same age who may have lost interest in this type of material. A general guideline concerning age appropriateness of materials is to consider whether or not someone else of the same age would be interested in interacting with the material.

Of course, a great deal of literacy materials can extend across a relatively wide age range (e.g., comic books, Dr. Seuss books, classic literature). The team supporting the student can work with the student and family to determine what is most appropriate and what will help the student make progress in this area. Intervention strategies may need to be developed to help a student explore more age-appropriate reading and writing materials and gain interest in these. It may be necessary to allow the student access to desired yet age-inappropriate material while concurrently introducing newer and age-appropriate materials. Matching certain characteristics of the less appropriate (younger) material with the desired material may facilitate the student's acceptance of and interest in the new material. For example, for the teenager who seems to prefer only Barney-related material, replacing it with books related to dinosaurs or to pictorial information that contains a lot of the color purple (e.g., sports outfits) may entice him to investigate the new material. Peers can be instrumental in facilitating this transition through their own enthusiasm and interest in more meaningful and age-appropriate reading material.

The plethora of magazines on the market targeting an extreme diversity of topics and filled with colorful photographs present a relatively easy way to provide age-appropriate reading materials. Literature on commercial CDs and DVDs provide voice output and colorful pictures and, at times, video clips. This multimodal approach to literature may make it more feasible to provide interesting reading material that is age appropriate as well. Helping students explore a wide range of age-appropriate materials should be a major goal of all team members so that the student can increase access to more information and entertainment.

Students with significant disabilities who show interest in broader and more age-appropriate material are demonstrating progress in literacy.

Individual Considerations

When a student has specific disabilities, certain accommodations will be necessary to make the material accessible. Physical and sensory disabilities will require adaptations. The student's cultural views and background also need to be considered when planning appropriate literacy activities.

Physical Considerations

The amount of physical control and movement will impact literacy activities and materials. Of primary importance is a stable and comfortable position in which to engage in literacy activities. Students should be properly supported in any position that will allow them to access literacy materials (e.g., sitting, kneeling, standing, lying down) as well as close access to peers. Such support could be provided by an adult, for example, when a child is held next to or on a lap, or by specific positioning equipment. While holding a young child on your lap is feasible, it is more difficult to see facial expressions, and hands may be more constrained. Therefore sitting next to a child may be more practical. Positioning equipment for students unable to sit or stand independently may include a corner chair; customized wheelchair; Rifton chairs; upright, prone, and supine standers; or a variety of bolsters and wedges. The unique physical needs of each student will determine the most effective positioning equipment. Since students need to change their positions frequently, several pieces of equipment may be needed for each student. Some equipment can be particularly bulky and large, and care needs to be taken to ensure that its use does not isolate the student from classmates. Careful consideration of how equipment is used and placed within a classroom is needed, as well as encouraging other students to get close to the student using the equipment. The primary purpose of effective positioning is to make the student comfortable and provide the most efficient access to meaningful materials and active participation in activities throughout the day (Beukelman & Mirenda, 1998; McEwen, 1997).

Once optimal positioning has been achieved, reading and writing material will need to be brought within the reach of the student to avoid overtiring the child. Homemade or commercial slant boards elevate the material, making it easier to visually and physically access. Universal mounts attached to wheelchairs can bring material within the visual and

Figure 3.2   Homemade Page Fluffers Using Chunks of Dried Sponge to Separate Pages

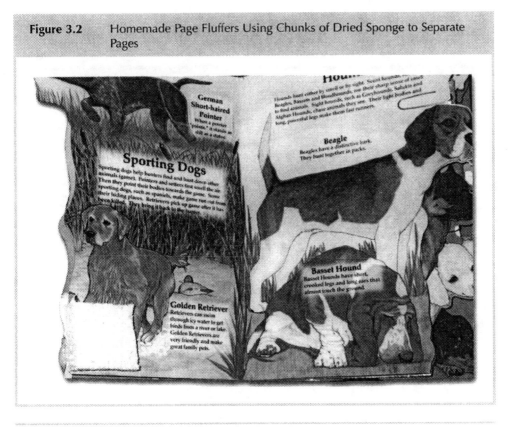

SOURCE: Nayer, Judy, *Dogs and Puppies at Your Fingertips*. Used with permission from the author.

physical reach of a child without the need of a table or a tray. Page fluffers or adapted page turners added to pages separate the pages, making them easier to turn. See Figure 3.2 for an example of this homemade adaptation using dried sponges. Commercial page turners activated by a switch are available to allow for independent turning of pages that are beyond the student's ability to do so.

A variety of adapted grippers for writing implements (pens, pencils, crayons, markers, paintbrushes) are designed to enhance the student's ability to grasp these implements and support writing practice. Figure 3.3 provides different examples of some commercially made adapted grippers for students with limited fine motor control of their hands. Similar adapted grippers can be inexpensively made using old racquet balls, play dough, or a washcloth wrapped around a writing tool. Students who have greater control of their oral musculature and head movements can use a head pointer/gripper or mouthpiece with which to write. Writing and reading material may need to be firmly fastened in such a way so as

Figure 3.3   Commercially Produced Adapted Grippers

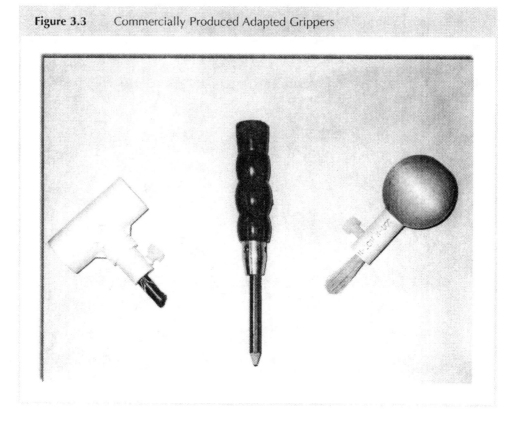

to prevent slippage and keep pages from turning too soon. Papers can be taped down on the desk or table, and a simple adaptation with rulers and tape can be used to hold a book flat and open on a given page. A clipboard also can be used to hold paper in place or to hold a book or magazine page open. For students accessing the computer or augmentative communication devices to compose messages, a hand or head or mouth pointer can be used for clearer identification of the desired symbols.

Students having limited motor control or movement can make use of switches and switch-activated devices for reading and writing activities (see Elder & Goossens, 1996; Musselwhite & King De-Baun, 1997). Students can activate a switch to listen to a book on tape or electronic book on the computer. A rotary scanner with pictures and words can be activated with a switch, allowing the student to select answers to questions asked. A student can use a switch to operate a slide projector to tell a story or give a report. Switches can be interfaced with a number of devices that allow a student with minimal movement to actively engage in a wide variety of activities.

Visual Considerations

Students with significant and multiple disabilities often can have visual impairments as well. Students who have remaining functional vision may need materials to be bigger; utilize clearer spacing between letters, words, or pictures; contain less detail (e.g., shadowing effects) or bolder lines; or appear in a certain visual field. Magnifying aids are available commercially to enhance the size of text and pictures, and copying machines can easily enlarge information. Decisions need to be made as to whether the addition of color will increase understanding or be more confusing to a student. Background typically should be of less visual interest (dull, plain) so as not to compete with the important visual information presented. For example, if a picture of a clear glass of water is affixed to a bright solid red backing, the student with severe visual and cognitive disabilities may attend more to the bright red background versus the representative picture. Downing (2003) and Kovach and Kenyon (2003) provide several examples of necessary visual adaptations to assist students with significant disabilities access materials in the classroom.

When students have no functional vision, so that print and pictures are not accessible, alternatives must be used. The majority of students with significant cognitive and visual impairments with limited language skills will not acquire the full braille code for reading and writing, which is more complex than standard print. However, they may be able to gain some skills with this form of writing to support their literacy efforts. Therefore braille should always be used in conjunction with print (for those who see) and tactile material for the student to read. Students read tactile information much the same way that students read pictorial or written information. They feel items on pages of books that represent referents with which they have experienced. Obviously, some material is easier to adapt with this mode than others; however, basing books on students' experiences is quite possible and makes for more meaningful interaction with the material. In Figure 3.4, a tactile book has been created for a young man based on his weekend camping trip with his family. Even though he does not know braille, he feels it and feels the representative item(s) on each page to learn that these both represent the story. By adding print and braille, those who have access to these modes can read the story with the young man. The print and braille on the page read, "I worked on my lanyard and then went to sleep. It was a fun time." The representative item is a lanyard.

When devising tactile books, items must be selected based on the student's personal and *tactile*, not visual, experiences. What is felt

Figure 3.4 Sample Page From a Student's Tactile Book About His Weekend Camping Trip

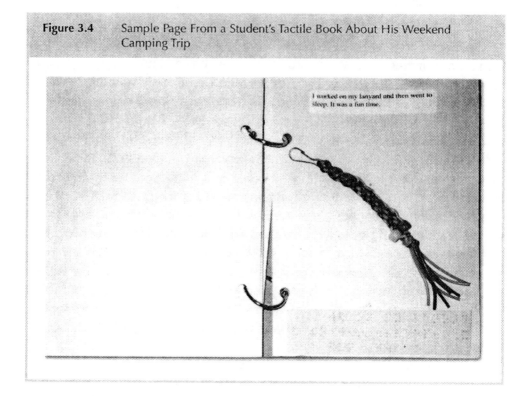

I worked on my lanyard and then went to sleep. It was a fun time.

by the hands may be quite different than what is perceived in total by the eyes. Furthermore, since the hands feel relatively small parts of items at one time, whole (and large) items may not be needed in the development of the books. Using the tactile pieces that are most representative from the student's perspective (e.g., this student doesn't see a lot of trees when hiking, but does feel small parts of bark on the trees) makes more sense. Small parts of objects determined to be most tactilely representative can be affixed to thick paper, such as pages made from file folders or thin cardboard. Any strong glue adhesive can be used, as well as Velcro or Handitak. Items difficult to adhere to a page can be placed in a baggie with the baggie stapled to the page. These items can be easily removed to allow full exploration as needed. Adhesives typically take time to adhere firmly and may interfere with a clear tactile representation if the backing cannot be removed. While Velcro allows flexibility to add or remove an item to pages, it requires affixing Velcro to every item and, by doing so, can interfere with clear tactile recognition of the symbol. Handitak (or any gummy adhesive) is flexible and easily removed from the item for careful tactile exploration. However, it may not hold larger items as tightly as other means. As with photographs and drawings, tactile books should always have clear text accompanying the item(s) so that information presented is clear for all readers.

For those students just learning about objects in their world, creating tactile story boxes might be helpful. A copy of the book would go in the box as well as several representative items that will be brought to the student's attention while it is read. These items also can be used when asking the student comprehension questions about the story. For instance, a first-grade programmed reader about making and selling lemonade was adapted tactilely for a young boy with no vision, very limited speech, and physical disabilities. A box contained the reader, an adapted tactile reader with braille and representative parts of objects (e.g., lemon peels, sugar packets, spoon handle), and a small bottle of lemonade, lemons, more sugar, cups, and an empty bottle. Using the whole, real items in the story and paired with the tactile reader may help this young student grasp the concept of books and reading. For more information on devising tactile adaptations for students without functional vision, see Downing (2003), Downing and Chen (2003), and Lewis and Tolla (2003). American Printing House for the Blind provides tactile books and tactile book kits for students who are legally blind, at no cost to the school district.

Although very limited research has been done on the use of jumbo braille for students with significant disabilities, the use of this adapted braille may hold merit. Jumbo braille is substantially enlarged braille, making it potentially easier to tactilely recognize than the standard size. An example of greatly enlarged braille is the Tack-Tile, which contains one letter or contraction in braille on a Lego block. Figure 3.5 demonstrates the actual size difference between the standard letter "J" in braille and its jumbo Tack-Tile equivalent. Students with significant intellectual disabilities in addition to severe physical impairments that make it difficult to discern differences through the sense of touch may, in fact, make more progress with this adaptation. While some advocate its use in an attempt to support access to more conventional literacy for those students who are blind, empirical research has not been done to confirm this hypothesis. The real difficulty with introducing such a tactile accommodation is its extremely limited availability. Most commercial material does not use this format, and only those few professionals with access to a jumbo braille embosser (e.g., equivalent to a printer) or jumbo brailler, which equates to a typewriter, would be able to ensure its use on a consistent basis. Obviously, research is needed in this specific area to determine its effectiveness and overall usefulness.

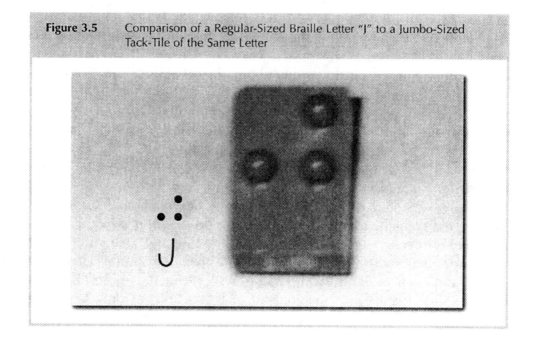

Figure 3.5 Comparison of a Regular-Sized Braille Letter "J" to a Jumbo-Sized Tack-Tile of the Same Letter

Cultural Considerations

Considerable attention has been paid to the need to recognize and respect the different cultural values and beliefs that individual students have (Neuman, 1999; Rossi, 2000). Cultural differences have been found concerning the perceptions of graphic symbols (Huer, 2000) and what types of AAC devices should be used (Parette, Chang, & Huer, 2004). Different cultural experiences may account for the different ways in which symbolic material is perceived, which may interfere with effective teacher-student understanding. Whether significantly disabled or not, all students have the right to engage with literacy materials that reflect their culture, language, and interests surrounding their culture (Corso, Santos, & Roof, 2002). Commercial books have become much more responsive to this need, and copies of pictures from such books may be of particular value for students who need pictorial support. Photographs of the student and his or her family can be used for reading and writing activities, which will naturally reflect the culture of the student. Certainly, families can help guide the process of selecting and using materials that reflect cultural diversity (Corso et al., 2002). Peers also can be instrumental in explaining cultural differences and providing interpretations for different words or phrases. In this way, materials will be individualized for the student and reflect the many different ways in which each student has diverse needs and interests. In addition, the languages experienced by the student should be reflected on materials being used. Some software programs that provide graphic symbols also make it possible to label the symbols in a variety of different languages (e.g., Boardmaker by Mayer-Johnson or IntelliPics). Adding both languages needed may assist the student in identifying the symbol and may help family members read material with their children.

Interesting Material

For material to be of interest to the student, it must be meaningful. To help beginning readers with significant disabilities understand the value of books and other literacy materials, it will be important to make the material as interesting and relevant as possible (Allington & Baker, 1999; Fisher & Kennedy, 2001). Students need to be given choices of materials they would like to read and topics that they would like to write about. Offering students choices helps identify what is interesting to students who may not be able to verbally articulate interests. Commercial material is available in a variety of topics that can be used with all students able to access the information. Materials that are handmade can be based on the life experiences of the student to make them relevant and easier to understand. Photograph books, drawings, or tactile books can provide the illustrations for a story line that is recognizable to the student and therefore supports the learning of the accompanying text.

When using pictorial information to support the access to print, decisions will be needed regarding not only what visual information to use but also how much. While some computer software programs (e.g., Writing with Symbols by Mayer-Johnson) may produce a graphic symbol per word typed, such information may be too abstract as well as too visually confusing to be helpful. Deciding what pictorial information to add to the text to make the information meaningful and interesting, while avoiding visual clutter, will need to be individually determined per student.

When using tactile information for students who do not use vision, it is important to ensure that the material is meaningful from a tactile perspective. Decisions will need to be made regarding what information *can* be made meaningful given tactile input. For example, colors, rainbows, extremely large items (airplanes, skyscrapers), and extremely small items (microbes, fleas) will be difficult to adapt for a tactile learner who also has intellectual impairments and limited language skills. Therefore not all information will be adapted. To prepare for a student in a second-grade class who needed tactile input, a worksheet with a blank line preceding a noun for students to write an appropriate adjective was adapted to include only adjectives that could be tactilely represented (e.g., soft, furry, smooth, rough). Color words and more abstract adjectives and nouns were omitted. Textures representing these adjectives (e.g., cotton balls for soft, small piece of tile for smooth, roofing tile for rough) were provided to the student along with an item (e.g., cup, stuffed animal). The student was taught to match the texture to the item (e.g., smooth tile with the cup). The texture (adjective) selected was affixed to the worksheet by the appropriate noun and turned in with the rest of the class papers.

High Quality

Literacy materials that are engaging, entertaining, meaningful, and fun to read will enhance the literacy experience. Certainly, some reading material is better than others. The construction of the story should be interesting, not too challenging for the student, and have accompanying illustrations that add to the story line. Materials that are handmade should be well constructed, durable, well designed, and inviting to a range of students (those with and without disabilities). Care should be taken so that not too much information is on one page and the book is not too difficult to handle (hold and turn the pages). Gately (2004) recommends putting limited print that clearly goes with pictorial information on the same page for the reader to more easily make the picture-text association. Audiotaped material should have interesting voices that are entertaining to listen to and at a good pace. Audiotapes should be of good quality, clear, and have limited background noise. A host of educational software programs are commercially available that can increase the motivation to engage in literacy activities. Programs should be individually selected for students based on their ease of access, clarity, age appropriateness, and interest level. In other words, students without disabilities enjoy materials that are of high quality, and the same can be said for students with significant disabilities.

Assistive Technology

The abundance of assistive technology available to support literacy skills development of students with significant disabilities is promising. Students can make use of simple switch technology to operate recorded material and follow along with written/pictorial or tactile material. Unfortunately, students with the most significant disabilities may have limited access to the more sophisticated technology they need (Erickson &

Koppenhaver, 1998; Harding, 2003; Koppenhaver, Erickson, & Skotko, 2001). The presumption of incompetence, of not being able to make use of the assistive technology, creates a serious barrier to developing critical skills. Students can't demonstrate the skills to show what they know without the assistive technology, yet they may not be provided with the necessary technology because they can't demonstrate basic skills to use it. This Catch-22 condition places the student in an impossible situation and is analogous to withholding books from first graders because they do not know how to read.

Giving students the necessary technology and then teaching them how to use it is a critical responsibility for all educational team members. As Koppenhaver (2000) states, "Children's demonstration of emergent literacy learning seemed much less dependent on cognitive capability than on learning opportunity, modeling of possible uses of print and communication symbols, and access to supportive texts and technologies" (p. 273). Negative attitudes and low expectations must be overcome to provide these students with the technology that will support their continued growth. Maybe the student won't be able to make use of all aspects of the assistive device. However, many of us make use of various electronic devices and yet never use them to their full potential. We may never master them, but that does not mean that they do not fulfill a need. We become more capable with continued use. Without consistent and ongoing opportunities to take advantage of what is possible, students with the most severe disabilities do not even have the chance to learn.

Computer Access

Students with significant disabilities will need specific accommodations to access computer programs. Fortunately, several high-quality products exist for this use. Simple switches and switch interface devices can be used to help students bypass the traditional keyboard and use a simple physical action on a switch to control specially designed programs. Using IntelliKeys with IntelliTools Overlay Maker, the entire adapted keyboard can become one large touch switch that matches what the student sees on the computer screen. More complex overlays can be made that correspond with a story that is being read or with writing options on the screen. The student makes choices of continuing to read a story, rereading part of the story, or making creative sentences by touching the matching symbols on the adapted keyboard. See Figure 3.6 for a sample writing overlay. In this manner, both the physical and cognitive challenges of accessing a computer are reduced.

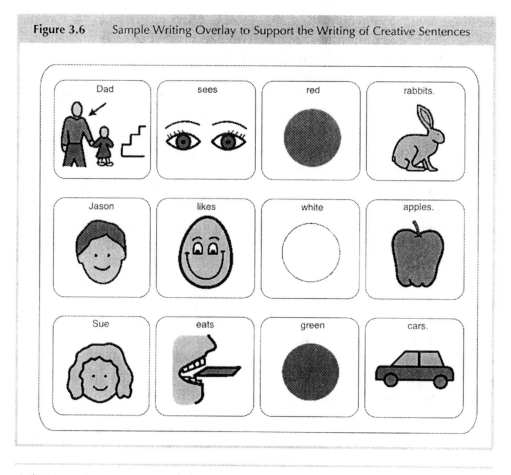

Figure 3.6 Sample Writing Overlay to Support the Writing of Creative Sentences

© The Picture Communication Symbols.

SUMMARY

This chapter has focused on preparing for the instruction of literacy skills. Considerable thought, time, and effort are needed to make it possible for students with the most significant types of disabilities to have meaningful access to literacy materials and activities. A coordinated effort by all team members will be needed to determine important literacy goals, to provide opportunities to engage in literacy activities across the school day, and to develop the necessary and highly individualized materials. Family support is essential, since much of what the student may be reading and writing about will probably be based on events happening after school and on the weekends. Using materials supplied from the family will be most meaningful and familiar for the student.

However, the best material in the world and the greatest preparation will not suffice. The student will need structured and systematic instruction to gain the greatest benefit. Such strategies, which involve a team approach to effective intervention, are discussed in Chapter 4. The reader will find specific examples of literacy activities and instructional practices for different students.

FREQUENTLY ASKED QUESTIONS

1. Making adaptations takes a great deal of time. How can I keep on top of this when I have students in so many different classes?

Making adaptations for individual students does take a long time, especially when you are just beginning to do this. Trying to adapt all material at once for all students in all classes will be impossible. Therefore it will be necessary to take beginning steps and do what you can in the most efficient manner. Making adaptations is definitely a team effort (or should be), and no one member of the team should feel responsible for making everything that is needed.

A first step may be to find out who can help. Family members, classmates, paraprofessionals, related service providers, and volunteers all can be helpful in gathering the necessary materials (pictures, items) for the adapted material that needs to be made. Asking for help in obtaining the materials may be an important first step. Find out whether someone in the district has already adapted material for different lessons. Teachers cover fairly standard curricula at different grades, so an adaptation may already have been made for a specific unit or story. Certainly, once adaptations have been made for a given student, these should be saved and shared with others in the school and district so that each special educator is not re-creating accommodations for each new student.

Oftentimes a paraprofessional may be assigned to a given student in a general education classroom and may not need to be working with the student all of the time. In fact, it is a recommended practice that paraprofessionals not remain too close to a target student, but work with different students or do other tasks (Giangreco et al., 1997). Careful planning can make it possible to have the paraprofessional work on necessary adaptations during those times when he or she does not need to be directly instructing a given student. Most paraprofessionals would rather stay busy during the workday, and so making valuable material for a student would be a good use of their time.

Considerable lessons have already been adapted and are available free of charge from the Internet. Teachers can take advantage of what has already been created, knowing that adaptations of what has been adapted will probably be necessary. For example, IntelliTools and Ablenet (www .ablenetinc.com) offer teachers the option of downloading lessons that have been adapted using their software. This can create a considerable time-saving measure for teachers and all team members.

In general, it is important to realize that everything will not be perfect for a given student from the first day of school. There will be times when adapted materials are quickly attained or created, and other times when they are not as readily available. Teaching is not a perfect science, and this is true for all students.

2. How do I get team members to work with the student in the general education classroom without pulling him or her out to work on discipline-specific objectives?

Working in a collaborative and integrated manner as a team takes time and effort and a shared vision. Similar training and experiences across disciplines would be helpful in this process of collaboration. However, this is rarely the case. Typically, specialists providing related services are trained according to discipline-specific guidelines and do not receive much instruction in the area of role release or integrative service delivery (Giangreco, Edelman, Nelson, Young, & Kiefer-O'Donnell, 1999; Utley & Rapport, 2000).

Helping everyone remember the goals of inclusive education and the benefits that the student gains from learning with his peers is important. All team members must keep their focus on the bigger educational picture for the student and not on discipline-specific skills that may or may not be important for the student. Skills learned in isolation of a natural environment, no matter how skilled the therapist, will need to generalize to the actual environment in which the skills are most needed. By teaching skills as part of important activities within the classroom that the student naturally experiences, the student does not need to learn skills in one environment with one set of stimuli and then transfer them into the more natural environment. While teaching the student certain skills during the course of typical classroom activities may require related service providers to rethink strategies traditionally employed in isolated, unnatural contexts, the end result should be more effective for the student. For example, sitting in a therapy room responding to direct questions to point to certain pictured items may help the student recognize vocabulary, but such a skill is of little use if the pictured items are not vocabulary needed by the student during the school day. Learning to recognize (and use) pictured items during meaningful activities as they naturally occur would seem to make much better use of a skilled service provider than a more isolated approach. Helping everyone on the team recognize the important and integrative role played by all team members may help encourage greater collaboration.

Teaching Literacy Skills

- Making literacy learning appropriate for students with significant disabilities means providing choices of materials, following the students' interests, increasing the number of meaningful opportunities, and ensuring accessibility.
- Isolated and out-of-context instruction is not recommended.
- Practical literacy learning opportunities involve using a daily planner, following in-task directions, self-monitoring, and sharing personal experiences.
- Instruction should be fun and interactive and teach skills within an obvious context.
- Specific instructional strategies include drawing attention to the natural stimulus, modeling the desired behavior, waiting for a response, and providing corrective feedback and praise.
- Checking for comprehension is essential and ensures active involvement of the student.
- Supports should be faded over time, while facilitating the generalization of skills to different tasks and environments.

There are many different ways to teach students literacy skills. No single approach will work with every child. This is particularly true when students have quite different ways in which they interact with and act upon their world. When students have complex communication needs, difficulty moving their bodies, and are not receiving typical visual and/or auditory information, teachers will need to develop unique ways of making literacy a feasible goal. Despite unique differences in how these students learn, there are some general strategies that should be considered by all teachers to make literacy accessible and meaningful. Suggestions offered in this chapter will include strategies to consider for all students as well as some specific strategies and accommodations for individual students with quite complex needs.

CONCERNS WITH SOME PAST PRACTICES

While relatively limited research has been done with students having significant disabilities and literacy, the majority of such research has focused on isolated, decontextualized, and discrete practice of single literacy skills, such as letter recognition and letter-sound association (Browder & Lalli, 1991; Erickson, Koppenhaver, & Yoder, 1994; Katims, 2000). Students well into their teens and older may be required to repeat instructional lessons on basic skills they were unable to acquire at a much younger age. Such instruction has a tendency to separate them from same-age peers in an effort to remediate deficit skill areas (Kliewer, 1998; Kliewer & Landis, 1999). Unfortunately, little evidence exists to support such practices if the goal is to help students develop literacy skills that will generalize to meaningful environments.

Rote drill and practice of isolated skills (e.g., letter identification on flash cards) tends to have limited meaning for students with severe cognitive disabilities, and interest in such activities will likely be hard to maintain. Even teaching supposedly survival words such as *walk* and *don't walk* will not be particularly useful unless the student is taught to see these words and use them in the context in which they appear (e.g., a street crossing). Furthermore, some students may never be able to master certain basic skills, especially if taught in an isolated manner and may, as a result, be denied access to more meaningful instruction. Requiring students to demonstrate their mastery over presumed prerequisite skills in literacy can serve as a major barrier to addressing more realistic and attainable literacy goals (Erickson et al., 1994; Fossett, Smith, & Mirenda, 2003). The intent of literacy instruction is not necessarily to teach a specified hierarchy of developmental skills, but rather to help students gain an appreciation of how literacy impacts and benefits their lives. The goal is to help students be as competent and literate as possible.

GENERAL CONSIDERATIONS
WHEN TEACHING LITERACY SKILLS

Instead of following a strictly developmental approach to literacy learning, an approach that is broader, more balanced, and recognizes the many aspects of literacy is recommended. This approach builds on individual differences, interests, and strengths.

Besides very specific instructional strategies, there are some general considerations that should be in place to enhance instruction. These strategies include offering choices, following the student's interests, providing opportunities, making literacy activities accessible, ensuring meaningfulness, making literacy practices interactive and fun, and having clear educational goals.

Offering Choices

Imposing certain materials and topics on students in an effort to teach specific skills may not be the most effective strategy to use. Usually, students have specific interests and preferences that can be used to make the learning experience more efficient and successful (Lohrmann-O'Rourke & Browder, 1998; Moes, 1998). Offering students choices throughout the day with regard to literacy materials to read and to write in will help give the student more control over these learning experiences and therefore, ideally, be more motivating (Swartz & Hendricks, 2000). For instance, during a Sustained Silent Reading period, students are to self-select a book and read quietly for 15 to 20 minutes. This is an easy time period to offer a student with significant disabilities a choice of a comic book, handmade book of his or her own experiences, favorite commercial book, or photographic memory book of a class project. The student may decide to read one or two or all of these books within this time frame. At times during the day when there is no choice of reading material and students are asked to read specific material in a chapter of a book, choices to be offered could involve the reading partner, the location in the room to read, a position in which to read (in a wheelchair, on the floor on a wedge, in a sidelyer, etc.), or how to do it (being read to, listening on an audiotape, watching a CD with headphones, or using an adaptation like Bookworm by Ablenet).

Choices also are available when the focus is on writing. At times during journal writing, students are encouraged to write about a topic of their choice. Therefore the student with significant disabilities will have the same option, which can be presented using words, cloze sentences, pictures, photographs, or parts of items. At other times, the focus is more constrained, and students are to write about a specific topic. When the topic is predetermined, students can still have choices regarding how they will write (e.g., with magnetic words or letters, pictures, cloze-type sentences, drawings they create, photographs, pictorial software programs, rubber stamps, parts of items). There are many choices with regard to writing implements alone (e.g., markers, stamps, battery-operated squiggle pens, pencils, crayons, paintbrushes, chalk). Furthermore, students can decide the material on which to write (e.g., dry-erase board, chalkboard, magnetic board, computer with accommodations, colored paper, unlined or lined paper, index cards, or notepads). Letting students know that writing can occur on a number of different materials, all of which are acceptable, gives them more control over the writing process. Thus they may be more willing to engage in this practice and find it more enjoyable. For instance, one young girl in first grade, Joannie, had previously been in a self-contained classroom for children labeled "trainable mentally handicapped." She had been considered the student with the most severe disabilities in the room and had not been given academic tasks to perform. Joannie was nonverbal, with a very short attention span and limited self-control. In her first-grade-typical classroom, she saw all of her classmates engaged in considerable literacy activities throughout each day. Initial expectations that were new for Joannie included sitting in a seat, following the flow of the class in general, staying with the group, and being quiet. It quickly became apparent that such goals were insufficient and were not addressing the skills she needed to learn. The special educator adapted material for Joannie using pictorial information to help with her understanding. Joannie demonstrated her understanding of the pictorial information and started attending to the written text as well. Although she couldn't write a letter and produced very uncontrolled marks on a piece of paper, Joannie held a pencil while doing tasks, probably in imitation of her classmates using pencils. Pencil and paper were always made available to her regardless of her literacy skills. When asked to write in her journal, she was given choices of pictures from which to select. She tended to select topics around her classmates, in particular, her friend, Monica. Initially starting with pictures and then fading to word cards alone, Joannie was able to complete sentences by using index cards placed sequentially in separate boxes following the sentence pattern of "Monica is _____." Joannie seemed to take great delight in choosing the adjectives (a choice of three) to complete the sentence, which were then read to her and written in her journal. She held a pencil but used the word cards to put in the sequential boxes to form her sentences about her friend. Forcing her to write on a specific topic with a specific format (pencil and paper) probably would have created a strong behavioral refusal and interrupted the literacy that was occurring.

Table 4.1	Practical Writing Options Using Photographs, Pictures, and Parts of Items

- Letter writing
- Shopping lists
- Notes to a friend
- Birthday cards, valentines, postcards
- Daily planner
- Recipes
- Step-by-step directions
- Gift lists for birthdays, Christmas, Hanukkah

In another example that shows the power of offering choices (and their importance), a young kindergartener with severe and multiple disabilities was given a crayon to scribble on her paper during writing time. All of the other students had pencils, but a fat crayon was considered easier for her to manipulate, as well as being colorful. Without speech, this little girl could not express her need to be like others, but threw a major temper tantrum in her effort to access a pencil. When she finally managed to get her hands on a pencil, her crying, screaming, and kicking ceased as she happily made marks on her paper. Presuming what will be best for a given child may end up being much more difficult and time-consuming than offering the child choices in the first place. Several different options for writing (and reading) can be found in Table 4.1.

Following Interest Level

Certainly, having an interest in a topic helps all of us attend to and learn what we can about the topic, whereas material we find uninteresting (and perhaps even boring) is considerably harder to learn. Forcing a student to engage in a particular activity against that student's wishes can create rebellious behavior, anger, destruction of property (the material we wished to teach), and can lead over time to a feeling of dread and avoidance when approached with the same topic. If we can present material in such a way that students want to participate in the activity ("We get to read now"), the result will be much better than if we force the issue ("You have to do this now").

Following the lead of the student as much as possible is recommended. For example, an elementary student with severe autism and no speech had a difficult time in large-group activities and did what he could to avoid them. Although he did not particularly care for sitting in a large circle around the teacher and listening to her read a story, he was very much interested in getting his own book and sitting quietly, looking through it.

However, when this occurred, he was forced to put his book down and join the circle, where he struggled and yelled and created a distraction by trying to get away. The paraeducator supporting him may have failed to see the bigger picture of encouraging literacy in favor of making him comply with the group expectations. However, as we age, we are much less likely to sit in a large circle on the floor listening to someone else read to us and much more likely to choose our own reading material and engage in literacy independently. When the student was allowed to select his own book, he was willing to sit with the group. Keeping focus on the ultimate goal of literacy learning and not on strict adherence to rules would have benefited this student and the entire class.

Giving students as much choice as possible within a particular activity, as discussed above, can go a long way to enticing the student into the activity. Certainly, using the student's interests as topics for reading and writing will probably be more successful than predetermining what the topic matter will be. One student, for instance, who had the label of "deaf-blindness" but did have some functional vision, resisted looking at most educational material. However, he had a fascination with death, in particular dead plants. When given the opportunity to write about dead plants, by drawing them, coloring them, and illustrating a story in that manner, he was very agreeable and quite creative. A story line was then added to each drawing he had created that was then signed to him. In that manner, he could connect his story (written with drawings) to the symbolic words in text and sign. Although the topic of dead plants was not a particular favorite of the teacher, this student's interest dictated the topic. Words like *dead, black, not, green, no,* and *water* were words that had particular relevance to his stories but could be used in other stories as well.

In another example, a young fifth grader with severe autism and no speech and limited literacy skills spent a fair amount of time breaking pencils and destroying papers when asked to engage in literacy activities. However, during the Daily Oral Language (DOL) portion of the day, his teacher would use grammatically incorrect sentences on the board that related to Allan's interest—motorcycles. Allan's task was to listen to the sentence that was on the board and to determine from different pictorial information what illustration would best represent that sentence. He would sequence these illustrations on a page, and the paraprofessional would write a simplified version of the DOL sentence under the illustrations. The specific words that labeled the pictures were pointed out to Allan so that he could see this print form of representation. Allan was also asked to sign his name to this paper before turning it in. He did this by choosing his name from three names on sticky labels, all of which started with A. Originally, Allan was choosing his name from three sticky labels that were very different and color coded; essentially, he had to recognize only the initial letter and the name in red, not blue. So, changing to names all starting with an A (all in blue) marked progress that Allan was making with letter/word differences.

Besides following interest in subject matter when possible, it is also important to recognize the length of time that a particular student can remain actively engaged in literacy activities. Using creative, interactive, and hands-on practices that are meaningful to the student may go a long way toward increasing the time that a student can stay on task. Sometimes, the student can do some very good work academically but for only a very short period of time. Respecting this characteristic of the student and having other activities (that may or may not involve literacy) are important. Forcing a student to engage in an activity that the student has determined is finished will focus all time and effort on the refusal to work and not on learning. No one wins. It may be possible to allow the student a calming break and then try to return to the activity or another related activity. The use of a timer to clearly delineate work and break times also may help the student remain on task. It is certainly possible to address very similar skills and use different materials so that the task looks different to the student. Doing the same activity over and over again with the same materials on the same topic can be boring and fail to hold the interest of any student. Reading and writing tasks become something to be avoided, and not engaging.

Providing Opportunities

Practice makes perfect, so the more opportunities for students to engage in literacy activities, the better. Opportunities for reading and writing experiences are plentiful in most general education classrooms. For students who may not be able to easily take advantage of these naturally occurring opportunities, effort must be made to bring them to the student. In addition to natural times during the day to read and write across all subject matter, additional opportunities can be created for meaningful practice. See Table 4.2 for ways to increase the number of literacy experiences.

Rereading material to and with students helps them become familiar with the material and is a recommended practice (Beukelman, Mirenda, & Sturm, 1998; Westling & Fox, 2000). Different reading partners can be used to add some novelty to familiar material. Different reading partners change the social situation and can highlight different aspects for the student. Older students in the school can practice oral reading skills by reading to younger students and students having severe disabilities. At

Table 4.2	Creating Opportunities for Literacy

- Reading daily schedule before each activity or class period
- Checking off each activity/class in schedule upon completion
- Reading steps within a specific activity
- Checking off steps within each activity upon completion
- Writing name at center to participate there
- Reading names on folders to find your own
- Reading messages on augmentative communication devices before selecting one
- Reading self-monitoring behavioral checklist
- Documenting progress on a self-monitoring checklist
- Tallying points in a game and marking the winner

times, students who do not have disabilities but may experience difficulty reading, such as English language learners, may gain some self-confidence by reading to students who do not possess the reading skills that they have. Both students can benefit from such a partnership.

Reading can be encouraged not only during class time but also outside during recess and any transition time. Students' attention can be drawn to written material that is on walls of their classrooms and schools. Certainly, accessing the library on a regular basis helps instill the value of reading and, ideally, can generalize to the community after school hours.

Making Accessible

Literacy opportunities need to be everywhere. Classrooms can be arranged to encourage students to engage in literacy practices with quality books and other materials easily accessible (Fisher & Kennedy, 2001). Students who have severe physical disabilities and those who are blind with additional impairments will have more difficulty accessing these materials, and so they need to be made more accessible. Accessibility can refer to physical and cognitive needs as well as visual and auditory. Accommodations will be needed when, for any reason, the student is unable to access the materials in the same way as fellow classmates.

For example, Michael is a 5-year-old boy who has a terrific smile, loves music, loves to tease, and has devoted parents and a twin brother. Michael is also blind, hearing impaired, cognitively delayed, and uses a wheelchair. In his kindergarten class, there is an emphasis on active learning, and learning basic literacy skills is fundamental to class activities. Once a week, his teacher introduces a new letter of the alphabet to the class, and different activities evolve around this new letter. Students in this class produce an alphabet book of different worksheets they have done relating to each letter of the alphabet. Since Michael doesn't speak, write, or see, a different approach is needed. Michael is learning to identify objects that start with different letters of the alphabet as his classmates are learning to identify the letters and the pictures of items that start with that letter. Michael has a book with cardboard pages that contain different items starting with a given letter. For example, the "B" page reads, "B is for balloon, buttons, and Band-Aid." Some buttons, a balloon and, a small Band-Aid are Handitaked onto this page. The text is written in both print and braille so that Michael can feel that it is there as the page is read to him (just as children with sight see the print as they hear it read to them). Michael is asked to find each item on the page and is also asked simple questions about the objects (e.g., "What do you blow into?"). When producing the individual pages (worksheets) of his alphabet book, Michael was presented with different items, some of which started with the target letter of the week and others that didn't, and was asked to find certain items. These were then Handitaked onto the pages and were turned in to the teacher with the other children's work. Michael signed his name to these worksheets by feeling his name in braille as well as a shorter name in braille (e.g., Tim) and asked to find his name (the longer one). His name was then added to the worksheet. Due to the thickness of the various items, Michael's alphabet book was in different sections. That made it easier to handle, and he could take different sections home to read with his parents and brother. See Figure 4.1 for a sample from Michael's alphabet book. While every attempt was made to use the same items that were represented pictorially for Michael's classmates, sometimes it made more sense to use different items that were easier to represent and had more meaning for someone without vision (e.g., instead of using crayon to represent the letter "C," a comb was used). The skills that Michael was learning were targeted on orientating the book correctly, finding the symbolic information on the pages and identifying them, feeling the braille and learning that this is what is being read to him, learning initial sounds of certain words, and turning pages.

When students do not have the physical skills necessary to manipulate reading or writing materials, then accessibility will mean bypassing this limitation. Different mounts can be attached to wheelchairs or tables to bring reading material within visual range of the student. Simple slant boards (commercial or homemade) may elevate material sufficiently to make it visually or physically accessible. Electronic page turners can be employed via use of a switch, or a student may use a simple behavioral response (e.g., tap the page) to request a peer or teacher to turn a page. For

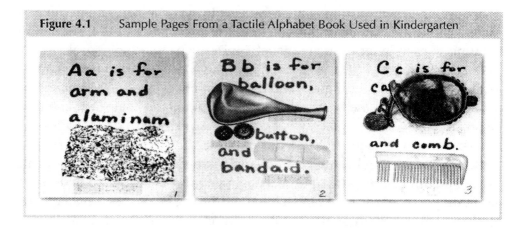

Figure 4.1 Sample Pages From a Tactile Alphabet Book Used in Kindergarten

students with some physical abilities of their arms and hands, page fluffers that widely separate pages in a book may be sufficient. Audiotaped books or books on CD can be switch activated to keep the student engaged in the reading process. A variety of hand grippers, as depicted in Chapter 3, ease the difficulty of manipulating a writing tool and may help provide the necessary support for a given student to express himself.

On-the-Spot Accommodations

Preparing the most appropriate and effective adaptations for a given student engaged in literacy activities requires preplanning and advanced knowledge of material to be covered. General and special educators need to work closely together to ensure that quality accommodations for a student with significant disabilities can occur. Although advanced preparation is always preferable, at times this may not happen. When plans change or whenever adequate preparation is not possible, teachers will need to act quickly to create the best possible accommodations.

To assist with on-the-spot accommodations, teachers will need to have immediate access to materials that can be used as consumables. Portable files of pictures organized by category (e.g., people, house items, toys, animals, transportation) should remain in the class where the student is learning or with the person providing support. Most elementary classrooms have glue, but if not, then glue and scissors need to be brought to the student for reading and writing purposes. Colored markers, highlighters, and pencils need to be handy to quickly add cues and assist the student with the assigned task. Sometimes other students in the class may be able to draw meaningful representations of material for their classmates who require information in pictorial format.

The following is an example of an on-the-spot accommodation for a third grader, Nico, who was nonverbal, used a walker, and was learning to read pictures. A sudden change in plans had the class reading the chapter in the social studies book on Canadian wood-carvers versus what had been originally planned. Although there were some pictures in the book, they were not sufficient to maintain Nico's interest or address his needs. A large portion of the chapter highlighted the making of totem poles. Instead of focusing on the geographical information or specific vocabulary related to carving and different types of wood, Nico's special educator focused on totem poles. She quickly found some pictures of birds, wolves, bears, and similar animals and also drew some faces with different expressions (e.g., angry, happy, sad). She labeled each of these and worked with Nico to create his own unique totem pole. Nico was offered choices of three different animals or faces, which were then pasted together in the form of a totem pole. Nico was also given color choices, which were also labeled using the corresponding colored pen (e.g., the color red was written in red). After he had created his totem pole, he was asked to find the various animals and facial expressions that had gone into making it. His teacher also used pictures in the book and asked him to find other totem poles pictured there, as well as to point to the picture of wood and trees. With relatively little materials, Nico's teacher was able to bring the novel content to his level of understanding, make it interesting for him, and work on vocabulary that could easily generalize to other situations.

Meaningful Literacy Experiences

One recommended strategy to engage students with significant disabilities in literacy learning is to ensure that it is meaningful to them (Connors, 1992; Katims, 2001; Kliewer, 1995; Kliewer & Landis, 1999). While many times, students with significant disabilities will be able to benefit from the same or very similar literacy materials, there are times when different materials need to be more meaningful. At younger grade levels, students may be able to understand the active and interactive nature of a number of stories and enjoy the sounds of words (if they can hear). In the upper grades, the increasingly abstract and complex nature of much of what is read can present a significant challenge to students who do not have symbolic language or the experiences to meaningfully access the material. However, there are ways to add literacy practices that involve very meaningful material and topics in a student's life. A list of potential reading options is presented in Table 4.3. These will have to be provided in a pictorial and/or tactile format to be understood.

Table 4.3	Practical Reading Options Using Adapted Material

- Menus
- Recipes
- Magazines
- Board games
- Letters/postcards
- Daily planners/schedules
- Cards in a card game
- Conversation books
- Directions to complete a task

The Use of a Daily Planner

A very practical and meaningful reading tool for all individuals is a daily schedule or planner. Most adults refer to something of this nature or an electronic device (e.g., a Palm Pilot) to help them organize and manage their days. Therefore it is a lifelong skill that can prove quite useful on a daily basis. Students with severe cognitive and additional impairments may find a traditional planner inaccessible given the emphasis on print alone. However, these schedules or planners can be adapted to make them quite accessible and usable by every student. Downing and Peckham-Hardin (2001) provided numerous examples of their construction and use for a variety of students with severe disabilities. Daily planners can contain photographic materials, pictures, or objects or parts of objects that represent an individual student's school day. While these planners or schedules often are used to help students anticipate and manage their days (Hodgdon, 1995; Schmidt, Alper, Raschke, & Ryndak, 2000), they also are excellent tools for meaningful reading and writing practice (Downing & Peckham-Hardin, 2001). Schedules can be in a book, chart, wallet, folder, slide holder, or any portable format desired by the student. Regardless of the format used, there should always be a print and/or braille message to be read per activity. This can begin as a single word representing the activity (e.g., lunch, recess, science, math) and then expanded to a short phrase or sentence as the student's skill level progresses (e.g., "Time for lunch" or "Yes! It's lunch."). Repetitive and predictable sentence structure (e.g., Time for lunch, Time for recess, Time for science) can be used to aid beginning readers (Gately, 2004). These sentences are changed as the student shows mastery to continue challenging the student's reading skills.

Besides the practice of reading skills that may start with one word recognition and expand to reading sentences, daily planners/schedules offer writing practice as well. Depending on the construction of these

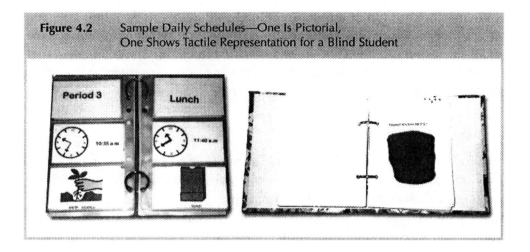

Figure 4.2   Sample Daily Schedules—One Is Pictorial,
One Shows Tactile Representation for a Blind Student

devices, students can engage in meaningful writing experiences that address individual needs. Students may use a dry-erase marker to place a mark on a laminated area next to the word or sentence indicating that the activity or class period is over. Other students can decide which of three prewritten words on Post-its goes with the activity and apply the correct Post-it label to the schedule page. A student with more fine motor control may use the written model on the schedule to write the word(s) on a laminated section of the page. Still other students may be able to fill in missing letters of the word(s) of the schedule page (e.g., the student writes in the "l" in the word "_unch"). Ultimately, the goal is for students to spontaneously write important words to manage their own daily planners. See Figure 4.2 for samples of schedules for students.

The use of a daily planner or schedule is described in the following vignette of Rosalie, a fifth grader with autism and severe intellectual disabilities. Rosalie uses a pictorial schedule in a book format that has a clear photograph of a single item that is representative of each activity of her day. A single word has been used to label each photograph, and pages are numbered to teach math skills. Initially, Rosalie showed little interest in the schedule and, in fact, would throw it or push it away when it was presented to her. However, the direct teaching staff (teachers and paraeducators) persisted and consistently presented her with the schedule prior to every new activity. Her attention was directed to the picture by tapping on the symbol and asking her to find what comes next. Using hand-under-hand guidance at her wrist, she was assisted to touch the picture, told what it was and what came next, then helped make the transition. At the end of each activity, Rosalie was shown her schedule again, told that the activity was finished, and was asked to take a marker and put a mark on the laminated picture. Such an action helped her structure her day, read the picture/word again, and learn the importance of "writing" (crossing out what is finished). She was then asked to turn the page to see what is next. Each step of using her schedule was systematically prompted, with a plan to fade prompts as she acquired greater independence.

Within-Task Directions

While a daily planner or schedule provides a meaningful way of reading and writing throughout each day, following written directions within a given task also offers meaningful literacy practice. Designed similarly to the daily planners, these directions for all or part of an activity are written simply, with accompanying pictures, photographs, or objects to represent each step. Steps to activities can be written down and provided to the student with whatever additional information is needed for a particular student. Sometimes all steps can be targeted, and other times, just certain aspects of the activity, such as clean up. See Table 4.4 for examples across the age range. This information can become part of a computer program for children interested in the computer (Kimball, Kinney, Taylor, & Stromer, 2003). The student reads each step in whatever medium and then engages in that step. Reading instruction occurs as the student is helped to understand each step. Words are highlighted for the student and graphics gradually faded as the student becomes a more competent reader. Directions can be very simply stated initially (two-word phrase, such as "Get paper") and become longer and more complex to encourage greater reading skills (e.g., "Get paper to write on"). As the student begins to associate the spoken word with the written word and the pictorial or object representation, components of familiar words can be further analyzed to address word-building skills.

The following is an example of a high school student with significant disabilities who uses tactile written directions for physical education (PE). Mahmood is a tenth grader taking a variety of different courses at his local high school. Mahmood loves to be outside, especially if the wind is blowing or if he can be swimming. He also loves listening to music and is quite adept at operating his own CD player. Mahmood is blind and has a few words that he says. He would be considered to have severe intellectual impairment. One class that Mahmood takes is PE. Like his classmates, he must go to his locker in the gym, change his clothes, and report to the gym teacher for class. To help him remember these steps, Mahmood uses a tactile checklist that has tactile dots added for the number of steps involved (e.g., 1–5). He feels the first step, which is a small lock and key. The print message, which is read by a peer tutor, says, "Open locker." The second step is represented by a collar of a shirt and a zipper on jeans to indicate the message of "Take off clothes and put in locker." The third step has a

Table 4.4 Opportunities for Using Within-Task Written Directions

Preschool	Elementary
*Snack time *Cleaning up after art *Morning-circle activities *Clean up at end of day and prep to go home	*Clean up after an art project *Math activities *Use of computer *Feeding the class pet *Recess options
Middle School	High School
*Getting materials for science lab *Doing different activities in PE class *Science experiment *Internet research in language arts class *Care of musical instrument during band	*Using a locker and dressing for PE *Preparation for art class *Taking care of plants in earth science *Use of computer in keyboarding *Workout routines in weight-lifting class *Office tasks for job experience

T-shirt collar to indicate getting into his gym clothes. The next step has a shoelace with the message, "Get gym shoes on," and the last message has the lock and key again to indicate locking the locker. Mahmood is learning to read his checklist of steps to follow and perform each step. A peer tutor reads each step, as Mahmood feels it to help him associate the "text" with the message. He also tactilely reads the sequence of raised dots to learn what to do in the correct order.

Writing also can be embedded within the use of such within-task directions. As individual steps are completed, the student can mark these off and proceed to the next step. Laminated sections by each step allow the student to mark each step and still have the directions usable for the next time. See Figure 4.3 for an example of within-task directions written for a student in a third-grade class that is studying the effect of combining different colors in science. This sequence of steps with pictorial cues addresses literacy skills of reading and writing (i.e., checking off each step when finished) and math skills of number recognition, number sequencing, and counting.

For students with no functional vision, magnets can be used. Magnets can be placed by each tactilely represented step, and the student removes the magnet after completing the step and puts it on the back of the schedule or in a small bag attached to the directions. For students who are gaining more traditional writing skills, important words can be left off of the directions, and the student fills these in before completing the step. For example, Bobby reads directions for making biscuits during home economics class. The directions have printed words as well as pictorial information. Each

Figure 4.3 Within-Task Directions for a Third-Grade Science Class

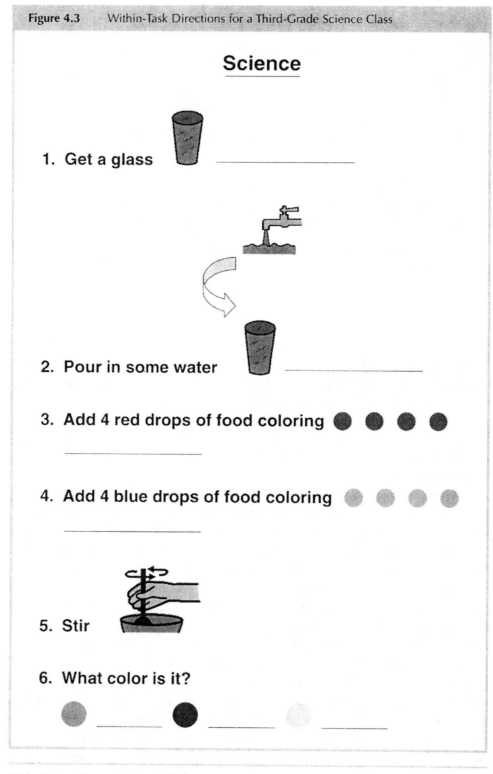

Science

1. Get a glass

2. Pour in some water

3. Add 4 red drops of food coloring ● ● ● ●

4. Add 4 blue drops of food coloring ● ● ● ●

5. Stir

6. What color is it?

© The Picture Communication Symbols.

step has a missing word that goes with the pictorial information provided, which he writes down before reading. He is currently matching the word from the pictorial information. However, as this skill improves, the pictures will be faded, and Bobby will be expected to write the necessary words from memory. Then, Bobby will read a pictorial clean-up chart to engage in those steps and prepare for the transition to a new class. A sample clean-up sequence that could be appropriate for a wide age range of students is depicted in Figure 4.4.

Figure 4.4   Pictorial/Written Clean-Up Checklist

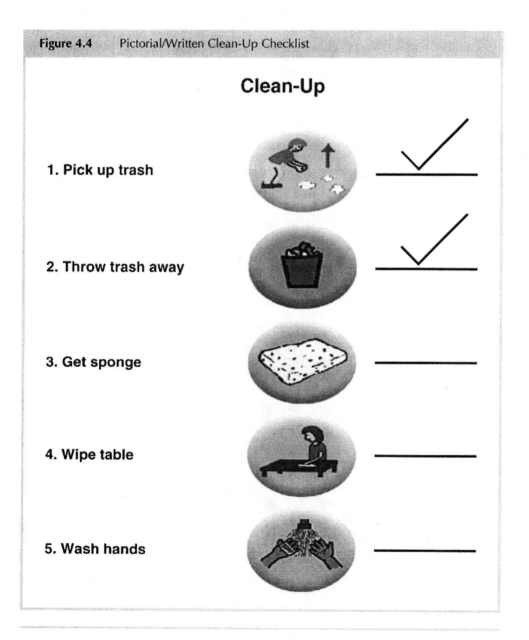

© The Picture Communication Symbols.

Self-Monitoring Checklists

Meaningful reading and writing practice can occur as students learn to self-monitor their behavior at school. Reading and writing instruction using self-monitoring checklists also teaches students self-management skills and makes them more accountable for their own behavior (Agran, King-Sears, Wehmeyer, & Copeland, 2003). Motivation to read and write using specially adapted checklists is increased if the student can see a tangible reward for demonstrating desired behavior.

Self-monitoring checklists can be very simply devised to allow students of a diverse ability level to access them. Pictorial cues and limited written words may be used to teach a student with minimal formal literacy skills. See Figure 4.5 for an example of such a monitoring tool. The importance of writing can be taught as the student makes marks to indicate the frequency

Figure 4.5   Sample Self-Monitoring Tool Used by a Student

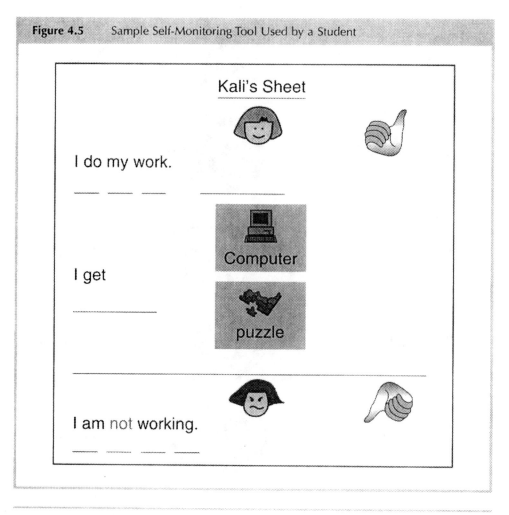

of the desired behavior. As the student becomes more familiar with reading this simple information, more words can be added, and more decisions made as to what needs to be marked.

For example, a first grader, Kali, is learning to stay on task for 10 minutes at a time. To help with this goal, tasks follow her interest level as much as possible, and she is given several options within each task. A timer is set to beep when 10 minutes is reached, and Kali is asked to read her chart and mark whether she has been working or is up and out of her seat. Pictorial information is added to the sentence, "I do my work" (a photograph of Kali working, a smiley face, and a thumbs-up sign), and there are designated spaces for her to make a mark accordingly. There is also a photograph of Kali out of her chair and under her desk, along with a frown face and a thumbs-down sign with the words, "I am NOT working." When Kali writes down four marks next to the "I do my work" message, she gets to choose a reward, which is also written on the chart with words and pictures. Her attention is brought to each word as they are read to her, and she is given her choice of reward, which is constantly changing. Systematic instruction of each step is needed to teach such skills to students with severe disabilities. Considerable time to practice these skills and receive ongoing feedback also is critical.

For students who can't access visual information, tactile checklists can be designed as well. First, the student's name is in braille on the chart for the student to read/feel. The student can make marks on the opposite side of the paper with a pen and over a plastic mesh screen. This creates a raised tactile line on the front of the page. Or the student can be given small magnets to attach to a magnet on the chart as a means of marking progress. A student also could use Handitak and place a small straight piece of pipe cleaner on the chart as a frequency mark. Whatever method is used, the student would write the marks and would count them to determine when a reward has been earned. The information would be simply printed and written in braille for the student to feel. The rewards would be represented by whole or parts of objects.

Language Experience Stories

Another meaningful form of literacy for students with significant disabilities is the development of stories based on their own life experiences. While not a new concept (Koenig & Farrenkopf, 1997; Neuman, 1999; Wood, Lasker, Siegel-Causey, Beukelman, & Ball, 1998), developing the materials to make them as accessible and meaningful for the student is somewhat more novel. Language experience stories can be exciting weekend activities or fairly common daily routines at school and at home. For example, the routine of walking home can be turned into an interesting story. For a student who is blind and has additional disabilities, walking home with his sister involves touching things he encounters. On one page of a story related to this activity, a flat piece of concrete wall is attached, with the caption reading, "There is a long wall on my way home. I run my fingers all along it until it is no more." Such text, which was created by his older sister, is much more interesting than, perhaps, "I touch this wall." The critical component is that the stories are familiar to the student who has recently experienced them. An example of such an experientially based story was given in Chapter 3 of this text of a young boy's weekend camping trip. Family members can help supply the photographs and tactile memorabilia that were collected during the outing.

Of course, language experience stories can be based on school activities as well. Various events (such as field trips, special assemblies, guest speakers, or class projects) can be represented with photographs or objects associated with these events. The documentation of these events helps the student remember them and participate in their retelling. While adults or peers may produce the actual text for the stories, when possible, students should be actively involved in developing the story line around these experiential stories. They should provide feedback as to how things will be expressed and in what order the pictures, photographs, or tactile remnants will go. For objects to have meaning for students, they must be held, felt, and tactilely explored during the experience. Then, once associated with the activity, they can serve to represent what was experienced.

Interactive and Fun

Besides using the most meaningful materials for reading and writing, teaching the use of these materials must be interactive and as entertaining as possible. Literacy is not a passive undertaking of being read to. Literacy learning for students with significant disabilities will require meaningful interactions between student and instructor and with reading material so that the student can construct meaning (Beukelman et al., 1998; Koppenhaver, Erickson, & Skotko, 2001). Teachers can add enjoyment to the reading process by using different tones and inflection, adding funny sound effects, making use of rhythm, and acting out scenes. As Gambrell and Mazzoni (1999) note, "Literacy is a social act" (p. 16). Encouraging students to work together should aid in everyone's understanding as ideas and diverse perspectives are shared.

Young children may enjoy learning about writing if they can practice in shaving cream, sand, mud, Jello, and water or something a bit more conventional, such as a magic slate that makes erasing fun. So many materials exist that have the potential to make the act of writing fun for a given student. Teachers and the entire educational team should strive

Figure 4.6 Three Fourth-Grade Students Sharing a Book

to be as creative as possible when determining which writing materials are possible and in offering students choices of those materials.

Writing activities for students that may be more interesting include quilt making, with each student writing his or her own quilt square; a story about the student's house, with different pages of the story making up the sides, top, and bottom of a 3-D house; and posters and mobiles of self-selected topics. Students can write by creating slide shows using Power Point and picking colorful graphics to accompany what a peer has written with text. Photographs can be taken by the student to create a story, and a camera can be switch activated to accommodate the physical limitations that a student may experience. A slide show using these photographs with prerecorded voice output also can be switch activated, further decreasing the physical demands of the activity.

Facilitating the interactions of classmates can add to the enjoyment of the activity as depicted by the fourth-grade students in Figure 4.6. Shared writing (Janney & Snell, 2000; Mather & Lachowicz, 1992) encourages peers to jointly write poems, stories, or reports, which turns literacy into a positive social interaction. In such situations, the more literate classmate may compose the actual text, while the learner with more significant disabilities decides the content, adding colorful descriptors and making decisions about illustrations, both pictorial and tactile. Both students sign their names and share the grade received.

Clear Literacy Goals in Mind

Teaching students literacy skills is challenging enough without having clear goals and objectives in mind. A plan must be laid to determine first steps and then where to go next as the student demonstrates progress. If goals aren't clear for the student, instruction may continue to repeat previously acquired skills and the student will not gain more sophisticated literacy skills. The development of individualized educational plan (IEP) goals should definitely reflect student and familial desires, as stated in Chapter 3. They also should reflect state standards in literacy, which may provide greater direction for teachers (Browder, Fallin, Davis, & Karvonen, 2003; Wehmeyer, 2003). In Chapter 5 of this text, examples are provided of IEP goals that are overly broad and vague and those that are specific, observable, and measurable. For example, the goal, "Roger will have access to literacy materials" is vague and not easily measurable. There is no criterion to indicate mastery or goal attainment. Clarifying what literacy material access will mean for Roger and what he will be expected to learn from these experiences is essential to provide effective instruction. If Roger is to make selections of literacy materials, turn pages, and respond to some basic questions about the material to demonstrate his understanding, then these skills need to be articulated in an objective so that everyone is clear as to the purpose of instruction. For example, "When offered a choice of three different reading materials, Roger will choose one within 5 seconds of being asked, then look at pages in the chosen material for a minimum of 5 minutes twice daily for a 2-week period."

DRAWING ATTENTION TO CONVENTIONAL LITERACY

Although emergent literacy skills are extremely important for students with significant disabilities, conventional literacy skills must be the ultimate goal for all students (Fossett et al., 2003; Koppenhaver, 2000). Therefore it is critical that students with significant disabilities be given specific instruction in conventional literacy skills. Some students may be able to identify initial letters to help them identify simple words. Some may be able to memorize a number of critical sight words that have relevance in their daily lives. Others will be able to recognize that words rhyme, and gain enjoyment from that skill while listening to a book being read. Since we don't know how much any person can learn, the importance of providing high-quality instruction is obvious.

Balanced Literacy Approach

Despite the limited research in the field of literacy acquisition for students with significant disabilities, including an intellectual impairment, the extant literature on the subject recommends a balanced approach for these students (Ehri, 2000; Katims, 2001; Westling & Fox, 2000). Students need instruction not only in the acquisition of basic skills (alphabetic and phonological awareness) but also in shared reading and writing, guided reading and writing, and independent reading and writing. Furthermore, instead of teaching word study skills in isolation, this teaching can occur within the larger and more meaningful context of reading and writing. For example, Ehri (2000) feels that reading and spelling are not two completely different sets of skills, but are integrally related. Even without all the underlying skills, learning to recognize some words can aid in the spelling of them as well. Instead of decoding the unfamiliar word using phonological attack skills only, recognition of the whole word may help the student identify some of the basic building blocks (e.g., letters).

For the most part, students with moderate-severe disabilities have experienced literacy instruction as isolated skills in a hierarchical approach (Browder & Lalli, 1991; Browder & Xin Yan, 1998; Erickson et al., 1994). For instance, students may be drilled on letter identification and letter-sound associations. They never reach a point in the instruction that allows them access to meaningful literature. Such instruction has met with minimal success and does not follow recommended practices (Barudin & Hourcade, 1990; Erickson & Koppenhaver, 1995; Katims, 2000). Perhaps students become bored with this type of skill acquisition and fail to see the relationship to more meaningful activities.

A more balanced and holistic approach is to engage the student in meaningful literacy activities and use that to highlight phonological skills. For example, as a student recognizes her name on her lunch ticket, math folder, science textbook, and other personal belongings, the individual letters are taught to her. As she reads about her favorite pop star in magazines, the letters and sounds of initial letters are taught. When she addresses a birthday card to her brother, she is taught the letters of his name. Nothing is taught in isolation, but the skills learned in meaningful words and activities are taught across different situations—different words. For example, when the student reads about pop star Britney Spears, she is asked to find the "B," which is also in her name, Bobbi. Time is needed for such skills to develop with many opportunities to practice.

SPECIFIC INSTRUCTIONAL STRATEGIES

Although children without disabilities may acquire many literacy skills almost incidentally as a result of quality literacy experiences at home, students with significant disabilities usually do not. They will need systematic instruction to help create greater awareness around the act of literacy, to learn that symbols can be used to represent thoughts, feelings, and events. Direct, systematic instruction has been used effectively to teach students with intellectual impairments to read cooking product labels (Collins, Branson, & Hall, 1995), picture/sight word recognition (Alberto & Fredrick, 2000), and reading for daily living (Lalli & Browder, 1993). This section will look at specific instructional strategies to employ with students having very significant disabilities who are just beginning to learn about their world and how to represent it.

Draw Attention to the Stimulus and Shape the Response

Students with significant disabilities won't have much opportunity to understand either the reading or writing process if they aren't made aware of the expectations. Several strategies can be used to help the student see the symbolic representation, whether print, pictorial, tactile objects, or braille. Depending on the student's abilities, verbally directing, pointing to the symbol, tapping it, adding highlighter or color, adding reflective tape and shining a light on it, and/or bringing the symbol under the student's hands can be effective strategies. Another strategy involves shining a light behind a picture to illuminate it and draw the student's attention. If the student looks just at the pictorial information but not the print, the same strategies can be used to draw attention to the print as well. This may entail moving print under a picture to above it so that the student's hand doesn't cover the print. For example, after completing a story in class, fifth-grade students are writing their reflections of the story. One fifth grader does not speak and is learning to recognize pictures and attend to auditory information. The story has been greatly simplified, with considerable pictorial information added to aid his understanding. Instead of writing a reflection paper, this student will be using colored pictures to fill in the blanks of several simple statements. The first statement is read to him, "The _____ went to school." He is given four clear and simplified pictures of a boy (which is the correct answer), a pig, and a house. As each option is presented to him, it is tapped, moved closer to him, and then read within the context of the sentence. He is given sufficient time to examine each option before being shown the next one. If he chooses incorrectly, he is provided with corrective feedback (e.g., "No, it's not the pig), and the correct picture will be moved closer to him than the other options. The line where the picture/word is to go is bold and highlighted to make that aspect of writing clear as well.

If the student reads objects, it is important to ensure that he also comes in physical contact with the braille, which may be more saliently placed under the item. Instead of manipulating the student's hands (e.g., hand-over-hand technique), a less intrusive technique of hand-under-hand guidance, or bringing the braille matter to the student's hands, is recommended (see Downing & Chen, 2003; Miles, 1999). Using auditory cues (e.g., tapping the object) draws the student's attention to the representative tactile information.

Model the Behaviors of Reading and Writing

Once the student's attention is on the representative symbol, then telling the student the word clearly and distinctly and repeating the information while pointing to the word (or mutually touching the item) can help support the student's efforts to associate specific content with its representation. In this way, the instructor is modeling the skill of reading for the student. Classmates without disabilities also can be very effective at modeling the act of reading and writing. Emphasizing the initial-letter sound while pointing to that letter of the word and using this sound as a cue to the student to read the word helps strengthen the acquisition of this basic skill. Words starting with initial letter sounds that are already in the student's repertoire may be easier for the student to make the necessary association (e.g., for a child who makes the "buh" sound for *ball*, highlighting the letter "b" in the word ball while showing the picture and the real ball may be more reinforcing than trying to recognize a more difficult-to-pronounce word).

For the student who does not hear, the addition of signs may be important (if the student is learning to use signs communicatively). Without knowledge of signs, the use of objects is recommended as well as acting out the meaning of the words. Students need to see, hear, and/or feel others "writing"—putting information on paper in whatever form. In general, it is important to make use of multiple modes of communication when reading and writing to support the student's understanding. Facial expressions, gestures, signs, pictures, and objects can all be used in combination with speech when teaching literacy skills (Beukelman & Mirenda, 1998).

Check for Comprehension

In many cases, the student may be receiving a great deal of information. However, this receptive understanding won't be known unless the student can indicate this knowledge. If the student does not speak, the easiest way to check for comprehension is to offer some options and ask the student to look at, point to, touch, or sign the correct response. Initially, options can be kept to two and gradually increased as the student demonstrates increasing competence. For instance, when reading his schedule, Brendon is asked to find the word *lunch* from two choices (*lunch* and *science*). Lunch may be represented by a picture of a sandwich, a tactile item (e.g., a sandwich bag), and either the print or print and braille under the object. As he consistently demonstrates understanding of the task, options will include three or four words.

Checking for comprehension is critical when reading material in class, whether for language arts, social studies, science, or any subject matter. Periodically asking students to confirm what they know about the subject being read (through whatever means) versus just passively listening and looking is critical. Cress (2003) warns that if students are just acted upon, they may learn that they are to be only recipients of information, versus learning to act on that information. Students can sequence pictorial or photographic material to retell the story. They can respond to specific questions about the characters or actions in a story with pictorial or object options that have been produced at a level meaningful for the student. For instance, one fourth grader who has significant cognitive disabilities has been reading the first of the *Harry Potter* series, by J. K. Rowling. While his classmates are asked to write creative alternative endings to this story or to analyze a character's actions, this fourth grader is provided with simple questions with pictorial format (Writing with Symbols 2000). Figure 4.7 provides a sample of the types of questions asked. Of course, similar pictures have been used throughout the reading of the story to this student so that he is familiar with them. A similar example of adapted materials required for a comprehension check is provided in Figure 4.8. This example depicts the questions asked of a student whose class was studying *The Legend of Sleepy Hollow*, by Washington Irving. The information has been made quite clear and simple with pictorial choices provided.

Another student in a high school biology class has very severe physical as well as cognitive disabilities and uses a rotary scanner with a switch to identify specific pictures related to the study of plants. He is learning to identify plants, dirt, water, and sun, which are represented pictorially on the scanner. He responds to specific questions such as, "We need dirt to grow plants, where is the picture of dirt?" His classmates working with him use his answers to provide more in-depth responses, such as the mineral composition of the dirt and how it promotes plant growth.

Wait for a Response

A clear antecedent prompt as a part of systematic instruction is the strategy of time delay (Halle, Chadsey, Lee, & Renzaglia, 2004). The delay

Figure 4.7   Adapted Pictorial Comprehension Check for the Story of *Harry Potter*

© The Picture Communication Symbols.

occurs after the natural stimulus has been presented and before a response occurs. This delay or wait time can be held constant between prompts, or progressively increased or decreased in length depending on the needs of the student.

Different students need different times to process the request, find the answer, and act. Being sensitive to the individual abilities and needs of students is necessary to provide the most effective wait time. Longer

Figure 4.8 Pictorial/Written Test for Comprehension of the Story *The Legend of Sleepy Hollow*

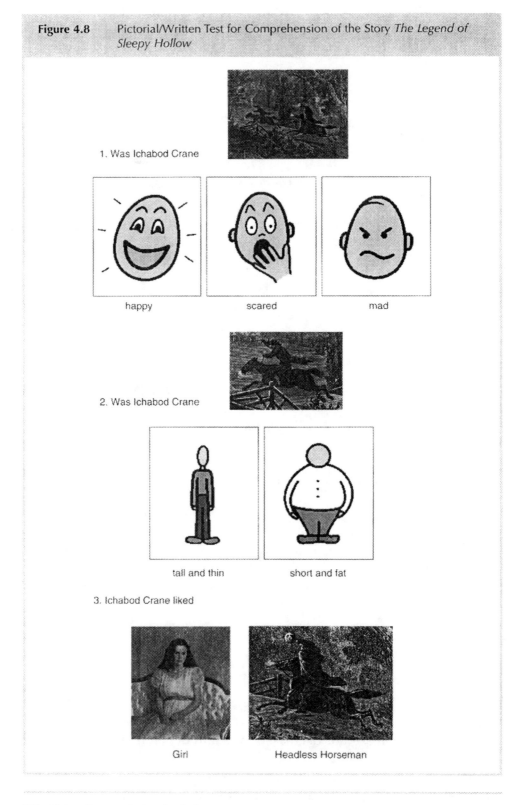

1. Was Ichabod Crane

happy   scared   mad

2. Was Ichabod Crane

tall and thin   short and fat

3. Ichabod Crane liked

Girl   Headless Horseman

© The Picture Communication Symbols.

response times may be needed for students with severe physical impairments and blindness. Teachers need to know the usual amount of time it takes the student to respond to a familiar and known request. Such knowledge will help determine how long to give the student before providing additional information. The wait time should be neither so long that the student forgets the request nor so short that the student has no real time in which to respond. As the student gains familiarity with the task and learns, the response time needed should decrease.

Provide Corrective Feedback and Praise

Sometimes, maybe often, students make mistakes. Mistakes happen with everyone, and so they should be anticipated. However, when mistakes happen, the student deserves to be told and helped to learn the correct response. If a student points to the wrong picture/word or touches the wrong object, the teacher needs to tell the student why the response is incorrect and guide the student's hand (or other body part) to the correct option. Providing information about the correct response and highlighting certain aspects of the picture, object, or word may help the student remember the expected response.

Correcting a student's mistake or lack of response does not have to be punitive or negative in any way. In fact, a negative approach is *not* advocated. But teaching the correct response is important and should be a standard procedure.

Of course, when the student demonstrates the expected response, immediate praise should be provided. To reinforce the response, repeating the words while pointing to them, touching them, and/or signing is advised (e.g., Yes, that's the dog!). Also, relating the words to the student's past experiences may help with recall and make them more meaningful. For example, when reading the page in a student's daily journal about walking his dog, when the student touches the leash handle, the teacher can say, "Right. You walked your dog, Sam. That's something you do a lot."

Being enthusiastic about a student's desired behavior relays the message that literacy skills, no matter how basic, are important and making progress in this area is something that should be celebrated. Progress of any kind should be met with excitement and outcomes that the student finds reinforcing.

Fade Instructional Support

Although students with significant disabilities may need considerable support to acquire even basic literacy skills, every effort should be made to fade the level of support so that the student can perform as independently as possible. Fading may involve waiting longer for a response, providing fewer cues, and fading pictorial information. To fade pictorial information, layers of wax paper can be placed over pictures or photographs until this visual information is very difficult to discern. At the same time, the print is kept clear and bold so that visual attention is directed there. Reliance on pictorial information is shifted to the printed text. Another way to fade pictorial information and highlight text is to embed the word in a pictorial symbol and gradually reduce the graphic information around the word until only text remains. Such a process of fading has shown some merit in shifting the focus to the desired text (Reichle, Hidecker, Brady, & Terry, 2004). An example of this fading technique for the words *orange* and *tree* are depicted in Figure 4.9.

Fading instructional prompts should be done in a systematic manner so that supports to learning are not removed too quickly and yet do not remain a part of the task when no longer needed by the student. Careful monitoring of the teaching process and the rate of progress made by the student should help determine when fading can occur and how rapidly.

TEACHING GENERALIZATION OF SKILLS

Research in the area of education for students with significant disabilities has indicated that unless specific plans are made to help students generalize what they have learned to other environments and activities, the chances of this happening automatically are unlikely (Browder & Spooner, 2003; Smith, Collins, Schuster, & Kleinert, 1999). Students will interact with similar literacy materials across a variety of different environments and activities. They need to apply learned skills in one environment and activity to other settings and activities. For instance, when a student learns to recognize the word *BOYS* on the restroom pass, the goal is that he also recognizes the same word on the bathroom door. This transfer of skills will need to be specifically taught to help the student recognize what he has learned and that it has multiple applications.

A student learning to recognize his own signature stamp and then using it to sign his name needs to be able to make use of this skill as the need arises. The same explicit instructional strategies used to teach this skill initially will need to be taught wherever this particular skill is needed until the student has mastered the skill regardless of the situation or circumstances.

Figure 4.9 Example of Fading Pictorial Information to Shift Focus to the Text for the Words *Orange* and *Tree*

© The Picture Communication Symbols.

One strategy to support the generalization of skills to multiple settings is to identify several different times and places in which the skill is typically needed. Although an IEP goal or objective may be written for a specific skill in a particular activity, if it is an important skill, it should occur several times in a student's day (e.g., recognizing one's name, responding correctly to comprehension questions). Identifying the possible times to practice specific literacy skills across the school day that go beyond what is stated in the student's IEP will provide more opportunities for mastery. Furthermore, when all members of the team are familiar with a particular student's IEP goals and objectives across all disciplines and subject matter, they can support the student's progress toward these goals and objectives by recognizing and using these multiple opportunities as they occur.

SUMMARY

Students with quite significant disabilities will need explicit and direct instruction in literacy skills to help them understand and acquire those determined to be most beneficial. These very specific instructional strategies are in addition to more general strategies that reflect best literacy practices for *all* students. Students with significant disabilities need numerous opportunities each day to engage in literacy and language experiences to develop these critical lifelong skills. More specific and conventional literacy skills, such as letter identification and letter-sound associations, are taught within the context of meaningful words and meaningful use of these words. Instruction also should be positive, with a focus on what students are doing, on their interests and preferences, and not on limitations.

FREQUENTLY ASKED QUESTIONS

1. The general education curriculum is way above the student's cognitive level. How do I make the reading material meaningful to my student?

Adapting the general education curriculum to make it meaningful and relevant to students with significant cognitive impairments is a challenge faced daily by educators supporting these students. Learning to extract the most critical information from curricular materials and bringing it to the level of the student takes considerable practice and is rarely perfect. Several resources exist that can support the educational team with this task (see Davern, Schnorr, & Black, 2003; Downing, 2002).

For students who have significant cognitive challenges as well as additional disabilities, extracting the basic information and relating it to the student's life experiences are essential. Taking this basic and relevant information and representing it pictorially and/or tactilely and with text provides the reading material for the student. For example, the teacher is discussing the establishment of the 13 colonies and the development of the Constitution in a high school American History class. In this class, William is learning about the American flag, which his family has raised on the outside of their home and car. William is learning the concepts of and words for the colors of the flag (red, *white*, and *blue*), as well as the words for *flag* and *stars*. While the class takes notes on the teacher's lecture, William is working with the speech-language pathologist on identifying the correct colors of the flag, identifying the American flag from very dissimilar flags of other countries, and completing sentences about the topic by picking the appropriate word from a choice of two. He does this by pushing a switch with the side of his head and operating a rotary scanner that holds a few pictorial/word options as answers. Sentences that he is completing include, "The American flag is _____, _____, and _____." "The flag has 50 white _____." "We fly the _____ at my home." William is not expected to learn about American history at the same level of understanding and complexity as his high school classmates, but he is expected to learn the most relevant information for him. Pictures and small flags are used as well as the assistive technology he needs (a rotary scanner and momentary switch) to be as independent as possible. A teacher, a paraeducator, or a classmate does the physical task of writing the sentences and gluing in his responses.

As another example, a middle school student who is blind and has severe and multiple disabilities is studying the pony express as part of a social studies unit with his seventh-grade class. This student will not be learning the routes taken by the pony express riders, the names of the major cities along the routes, or the speed at which the mail was delivered during the 1800s. Rather, this student will be introduced to the concept of horses, using real horseshoes, real horsehair from the mane and tail, hay, and alfalfa. A large bag will be used as the mail pouch, and he will learn to put the "mail" in the pouch and hand it off to the "rider." This student's vocabulary will focus on *bag, in, horse, food* (alfalfa), and *shoes* worn by a horse (as compared with his own shoes). When possible, a real horse is brought to the campus for the benefit of this student (as well as his classmates). As a culminating project, the class will write a report on the pony express, and this particular student will illustrate it using some of the items or parts of these items.

In general, adapting the curriculum involves identifying meaningful vocabulary and basic concepts, such as one-to-one correspondence, same and different, color identification, size comparisons, and following directions. The curriculum dictated by the particular grade and subject matter provides the backdrop in which to teach these skills so that students can learn together. For example, in the study of Anne Frank, a middle school student, Bethany, will not be learning about the war, Nazis, or concentration camps. Instead, this young lady, who has multiple disabilities and is just beginning to learn about pictures, will learn about the girl, Anne Frank, and her family during the reading of this story. Anne will be represented by a picture and a hair piece with a barrette (the paraprofessional or special educator will engage in hair brushing with Bethany when this is mentioned). Her father will be represented with a picture and a shaver (this scene will be acted out when mentioned in the story). Critical family members are represented in a similar manner. In addition, a blanket is included in this adapted story box and will be used to represent the concept of hiding. Other items that are discussed (e.g., Anne's diary, food eaten) will become part of this adapted story. Students in the class will help gather some of the items, which also will be used for another student who is blind with significant disabilities who will be studying Anne Frank in another class. Vocabulary, associations, and comparisons using these items will be targeted for the students who are not able to access the text.

2. My student doesn't seem to be motivated by anything. He shows no interest in schoolwork in general—certainly not reading or writing. How do I get him involved?

Occasionally a few students will seem minimally interested in things that most children express a great deal of interest in. This may result from a number of circumstances, including learned helplessness, extremely limited experiences, and extreme challenges in communicating preferences. In the case of learned helplessness, the student may feel unable to change any life circumstances, and for all intents and purposes has simply given up and assumed a passive role in life. Giving students a number of options and letting them understand that they do have control over as many aspects of the school day as possible should help reduce the effects of learned helplessness. Students must learn that their wishes are important and can impact what happens as a result, which means that those supporting students must act promptly and in accordance with choices made.

Extremely limited life experiences can leave the student with little idea of what is possible in the world. Interests can become extremely limited when the student is unaware of options. Obviously, the best practice is to ensure that the student is aware of and experiencing as many different activities as possible and at as early an age as possible. It may take many different experiences before the student is able to express interests. Of course, pairing pictures, drawings, photographs, and/or tactile remnants with these experiences is critical in order to use these materials in literacy activities later on.

Lack of a formal means of communication makes it extremely difficult to express interests. The difficulty that competent communicators have recognizing and responding to individuals who do not use symbolic communication has been repeatedly stated in the literature (Carter & Iacono, 2002; Kliewer & Biklen, 2001; Sigafoos, Didden, & O'Reilly, 2003). The student may have a very clear idea of what he or she would like to do but might be unable to convey this to those in control. If this situation persists over a long period of time, the student may eventually give up trying to communicate desires and just accept what others suggest. Such a situation is frustrating for the student and teacher alike. The first step in any instruction is to ensure that students have a way to express themselves. Communication is the key to any learning and certainly the basics of literacy instruction (Fossett et al., 2003). Communication modes do not have to be complex or expensive; they do need to address basic needs across any environment, and they need to support all areas of learning.

3. My student is tactilely defensive. When I present things for her to touch, she just pulls her hands back. When I take her hands to make her feel them, she screams and fights me. She's blind and nonverbal, and I don't know what to do.

Such a situation is certainly challenging. A student who is blind needs to use her hands (or other body parts) to serve the purpose of her eyes. Not wanting to touch certain things is not an uncommon problem, but certainly a frustrating one. Understanding what this behavior may be saying is the first step in providing positive support. Since labels have limited educational value, instead of labeling the student as "tactilely defensive," it might be more accurate to say that the student is hypersensitive or hyperresponsive to tactile information (Downing & Chen, 2003; Williamson & Anzalone, 2001). Each of us has things we care not to touch or have touch us (e.g., wool sweaters, slime), and with speech, we can make this clear and explain why. Without speech or sufficiently complex communication skills, this may not be possible. The only recourse is to resist having someone take your hands and make them touch things (e.g., the screaming and pulling back).

If the student had been forced to touch things she could not see, and did not see the value of this forced request, then over time, she may have become unwilling to touch new things. Certainly being forced to touch things one cannot see is not pleasant. Vision allows us to prepare for the tactile sensation that we experience. Without vision, there is no preparation other than what people are telling us. Trust becomes critical. Miles (1999) strongly emphasizes the need to be respectful of the student's hands and work carefully on establishing the trust necessary to facilitate the student's willingness to interact and learn.

Verbally prepare the student for items you would like her to touch. Let her know that you are touching the item and you find it interesting. If the student also cannot hear and does not understand symbolic language, touch the sides of the student's hands with your hands first and then slowly let the student feel that an item is there. In this way, the student can opt not to feel it and does not have to worry about being forced. The hands, especially the fingers, have many sense receptors and can be very sensitive to tactile information. It may be helpful to introduce the item to the sides of the hands or arms, tops of legs, or in the lap. In this way, the student recognizes that something is there but that it is her choice as to whether to explore or not. When she can tell that your hands are also exploring the item as it touches her, greater trust may be established and she may want to explore on her own. Instead of moving the student's hands to make her feel an item, push the item against the student so that she knows it is there and that she has the decision of whether or not to touch it. For students with very limited movement, it may be helpful to bring the item under the student's hands so that the student can feel your hands and, less directly, the item. Go slow, and try to put yourself in this student's position. Hands are this student's eyes, so think of how you would want your eyes treated.

4. My student knows his daily schedule—should I still bother with making him use one?

Yes! When a student knows his schedule, then it will make it easier for this student to start to recognize what is known as it appears in a written format. Although it's great that this student understands the structure of the day, that is only one purpose for having a schedule. Using a schedule or daily planner provides a very practical and meaningful opportunity to read. Other skills, such as identifying numbers, recognizing times of the day, and making choices, can all be embedded into a daily planner. When a student knows what is coming next, it's easier to help him learn to recognize the words in print. You may be able to fade the picture and highlight the word. If the student can't read the words initially, you can ask him what happens next. Then, using this student's knowledge of the schedule, help him recognize the letters of the word he thinks it is. If the student is just saying or signing one word (e.g., *lunch, recess*), then it's time to increase the written material to more than one word (e.g., "It's time for lunch," or "It's recess, yea!"). Understanding language typically precedes reading and writing, so it's wise to take advantage of the student's understanding of his schedule and put it to good use in terms of reading and writing instruction that has a clear purpose.

5 Evaluating Progress: Next Steps

KEY CONCEPTS

- Evaluation of student progress is critical.
- Alternative assessment procedures are recommended for students with significant disabilities, which include observations, checklists, and portfolios.
- State standards in literacy need to be interpreted and adapted for students with significant disabilities.
- Individualized education plan (IEP) goals and objectives should be clearly linked to state standards.
- IEP goals and objectives should reflect active student involvement, not something that is done to them.
- Data collection should be simple and routine and shared by all team members.
- Data should be used to alter instructional programs and determine next steps.

Ongoing assessment is essential to determine student progress and the effectiveness of the intervention program. Students with significant disabilities may progress slowly, and therefore it is critical to fine-tune assessment procedures to be able to document gains that are made. In addition, information on student performance helps identify strategies that appear to be effective, while drawing attention to those strategies that are ineffective or less effective. With this type of knowledge, plans can be made to alter the intervention and try another approach. Assessment data should not highlight student failure, but rather instruction that needs to be changed.

While standardized forms of assessment do exist for students with disabilities, they typically do not provide meaningful information for planning and often fail to identify a student's strengths (Erickson & Koppenhaver, 1998; Fewell, 2000; Taylor, 2003). Standardized forms of assessment often are based on a developmental model, which specifies which foundational skills will precede more sophisticated skills. They are often out of context and require a response on command, and the student with severe disabilities is either unable or unlikely to respond (e.g., identifying letters of the alphabet). Using such a model of assessment fails to capture what students with significant disabilities do know about literacy and what they can do given the necessary material and instructional supports.

ALTERNATIVE ASSESSMENTS

The inability of most standardized assessment procedures to obtain meaningful information and guide instructional practices does not mean that students with significant disabilities should not be assessed. Rather, an alternative method of assessment needs to be employed to provide the needed information. A variety of alternative assessment procedures may be used so as to gain a complete and in-depth picture of an individual student's strengths. Such assessment procedures will yield the most accurate and beneficial information if applied while the student is naturally engaged in literacy activities throughout the day. As such, this form of assessment should also be considered authentic assessment (Siegel-Causey & Allinder, 1998; Snell, 2002).

Alternative assessment procedures that have value for assessing students with significant disabilities include interviews with those who know the student well, observations of the student in natural settings, and review of past records. Samples of students' work can be collected and maintained in an individualized portfolio, which has been used effectively as an alternate assessment for students with severe disabilities to comply with federal No Child Left Behind mandates for accountability (Kleinert & Kearns, 1999; Siegel-Causey & Allinder, 1998; Thompson, Quenemoen, Thurlow, & Ysseldyke, 2001).

Interviews

Gathering information from those who know the student's literacy skills the best provides considerable data for determining present skills and planning future goals. Interviews done with family members provide information of literacy skills that students exhibit in their most familiar environment—their homes. The importance of seeking parental and familial input has been stressed as a recommended practice (Browder, Fallin, Davis, & Karvonen, 2003; Giangreco, Cloninger, & Iverson, 1998; Kliewer & Biklen, 2001). Family members can relate how the student expresses himself or herself and what helps the student understand what others say. They can describe augmentative and alternative communication systems that the student uses and how messages are represented for the student. They can describe how the child interacts with literacy materials and what their child finds most motivating. They also can provide information on how the family views literacy and what family hopes are for their child. Finally, family members can describe what interventions have been tried and the effectiveness of such past interventions.

Of course, the level of involvement by family members will depend on a number of cultural, religious, ethnic, linguistic, and personal belief factors. Families of different cultures typically differ on the level of involvement they choose (Kalyanpur, Harry, & Skrtic, 2000). Respect for each family's level of comfort in providing information and determining the family's level of involvement are essential. In addition, judgments regarding what families value for their child and their hopes for the future always should be avoided. Keeping families informed of what is possible without imposing certain values and expectations on them is preferable. Whenever interacting with family members who do not understand and speak English fluently, a qualified interpreter should be attained to maximize the exchange of information (Ohtake, Santos, & Fowler, 2000). Chen, Chan, and Brekken (2000) offer helpful suggestions about interacting with families through the use of an interpreter, such as making sure that terms used are understood, that questions and statements are directed to the family and not the interpreter, and that sufficient time is provided through pauses to allow the interpreter to stay with the speaker. Checking frequently to ensure that information is being shared accurately is imperative.

Interviews with past teachers, teaching assistants, speech-language pathologists, and others familiar with the student can provide information on what they have observed in educational settings. These individuals can describe how the student interacts with literacy materials while at school and what approaches to literacy instruction have been most effective. They can describe interactions with other students and the types of supports that the student uses to be most independent (e.g., signature stamp, specialized hand grips, vibrating pen). They also can provide information on what types of literacy activities and materials are preferred and hold the student's attention. These individuals also may have knowledge of previous efforts to engage the student in literacy learning.

Observations

Information from structured and unstructured activities provides authentic assessment of a student's actual performance under varying conditions. The value of observational data to obtain reliable measures of the student's actual performance, especially for students with the most complex disabilities, has been well documented (Blackstone & Berg, 2003; Browder, Spooner, Algozzine, et al., 2003; Clay, 1993). Observations can be made in real time as the activity occurs or from previously recorded (video or digital) lessons, which can be viewed by multiple team members at their convenience. The advantage of recorded observations is that team members can view the student in the same lesson either individually or as a group. Whether previously recorded or as the activity actually occurs, observational data can be very informative.

Observations should occur across different literacy activities and settings to obtain the most accurate assessment of the student's abilities in language skills, reading, and writing. Observations should occur when students are being read to, read with, and when they are independently handling literacy materials. How the student engages in reading and writing activities and what forms of literacy materials they use can be documented.

Observations also can occur when a student is being supported by a competent partner who can facilitate the student's active involvement. This type of assessment is referred to as *dynamic assessment* (Snell, 2002). Through this assessment, information can be gleaned from what is effective at supporting desired behavior, which can be tied directly to intervention procedures. For example, a young student may not be able to interact with reading materials on her own, but when seated on a teacher's lap with her body supported so that her head is upright and her arms are brought to midline, she looks at pictures in a book and will tap on a page to indicate her desire to have the teacher continue reading. Within a dynamic-assessment process, this type of support is noted for the impact it has on promoting certain behavior.

Review of Past Records

Careful documentation of past records and IEP progress reports should give some indication of a student's progress in literacy activities as long as the student was taught these skills. Absence of any reference to literacy skill instruction should alert the educational team to address this void. Reviewing past records should provide some direction for future literacy learning. Progress on past IEP goals and objectives that focus on literacy skills can guide the team in determining next steps for a particular student as well as identify potentially effective intervention strategies to use.

THE LINK TO IEP GOALS AND STATE STANDARDS

To be most beneficial, the alternative assessment used to measure progress and ensure teacher accountability should show a clear connection to the student's IEP. Furthermore, to keep expectations high for all students, the assessment also should be closely linked to the core curriculum standards in each state (Browder, Fallin, et al., 2003; Thompson et al., 2001; Tindal et al., 2003). Although these curriculum standards will need to be adapted to accommodate the needs of individual students, assessing student progress according to these adapted standards still focuses attention on standards all students are to acquire. The expectation for all students to be engaged in literacy learning is clearly present.

Adapting State Standards on Literacy

To ensure that we are holding all students accountable to approved state standards, we must make sure that in our interpretation of these standards for students having the most complex and challenging disabilities, we don't over-adapt and lose sight of the standard altogether. Standards will need to be interpreted for these students and restated so that they have meaning for the students and are attainable. However, stretching that interpretation so that the original standard is no longer recognizable misses the point. Browder and Spooner (2003) suggest that to avoid this overinterpretation of the standard, they should be written in such a way that general educators could clearly recognize them as pertaining to the original standard. If general educators cannot see the relationship, then they probably need to be rewritten and reconceptualized. For example, in math, the standard related to the ordering of numbers was interpreted for one student to mean that he would walk 3 feet in his walker independently, as measured by staff. However, this is a physical goal for the student, and although it may be quite important for the student to master, the relationship to the use of numbers as originally intended by the standard is not present. A more relevant math goal could involve matching numbers on photographs to a number line to tell a story.

The same pitfall can occur in the area of literacy as well. For example, for a standard related to the identification and use of letters as building blocks to create words, interpretation of the standard resulted in a student learning to grasp magnetic letters and release them into a bucket. Although magnetic letters can be used to teach basic literacy skills, in this example, the student is not learning to recognize the letters, but is simply grasping. Using materials that relate to a standard may be effective as long as it's clear that the underlying skill truly reflects what was originally intended by the standard. It is unlikely in either of the above examples that a general educator would agree that these relate to the standards.

The difficulty when interpreting core standards for students who are not demonstrating conventional literacy skills lies in addressing the basic tenants of the standard, while also individualizing for the student's needs. This is not an easy task, and each state has essentially been left with the task of doing this for its students with severe disabilities. There are few, if any, national guidelines. As a result, there is little continuity in how this is being done across the nation. Obviously, there is no right answer, and individual educational teams will have to work at aligning goals and objectives with the standards and making them meaningful for each student. In Table 5.1, some suggestions are provided for different students that might be helpful for individuals faced with this difficult task. These examples are not meant to be exhaustive and are only offered as ideas that may or may not

Table 5.1   Interpreting State Standards

Standard	Interpretation of Standard
*Identifies themes from a story	*Identifies the one object that goes with the story (after having experiences with this object during different readings and study of the story) from a field of 3 items
*Uses references to find information	*Uses a speech-generating device or pictorial card to request assistance when needed
*Writes a creative passage	*Uses IntelliPics Studio to choose different graphics to create a story
*Recognizes letter-sound associations	*Identifies own name from 2 very different-sounding names when they are both read with the first sound emphasized
*Writes to express self	*Scribbles a design or marks off steps of a pictorial checklist when finished
*Recognizes fact from fiction	*Identifies a mythical character from a story using pictures and a field of 2
*Critiques/reflects on a passage	*Uses a happy face or sad face to indicate like or dislike of a story read or will smile in response to the question, "Did you like the story?"
*Retells a story, getting the sequence correct	*Indicates between 3 pictures what came first and last
*Correctly responds to comprehension questions	*Fills in the blank of a simple sentence using the appropriate picture or object representation from a field of 2

be appropriate depending on the strengths and needs of students. However, even if the interpretation of the standard may seem beyond where a given student is performing, it is important to challenge students and to determine creative ways of helping students reach goals that at first glance may seem overly difficult. Providing the necessary supports and services will have a major impact on what students can be expected to achieve.

DEVELOPING APPROPRIATE IEP GOALS AND OBJECTIVES

To be able to adequately measure student progress in literacy skills acquisition, high-quality IEP goals and objectives must be written that target specific and meaningful skills for the student. Clearly reflecting family goals for their child, the educational team operationalizes these goals into measurable objectives. IEP goals and objectives should be written so that it is clear what the student is to accomplish and how the student will demonstrate mastery. Active learning by the student is essential (Browder & Spooner, 2003; Browder, Spooner, Ahlgrim-Delzell, et al., 2003). It also should have some social validity and be clear how the objective will lead to an improved quality of life.

Passive Versus Active IEP Goals and Objectives

When students with severe intellectual and other disabilities demonstrate limited responses to their environment, the temptation may be to write goals and objectives that do not specify active involvement (Downing, 1988). Rather, the focus is placed on what will be done to the student or, in vague terms, what the student will experience. For instance, a student may have an IEP objective written that says he will experience literacy activities. While well-intentioned, no information is provided as to what those experiences will be, and it is not clear what the student is to learn or how he will demonstrate what he knows. See Table 5.2 for examples of passive and broadly written objectives. Any measurement that occurs with these objectives relates more to what educational team members will do to the student than what the student is to master. In essence, these are objectives for staff, not the student. Objectives of this nature leave family members grappling with what instruction their child is actually receiving.

Active objectives, on the other hand, clearly state what the student will master as a result of quality instruction. Demonstrated progress is contingent on the student's performance of specific skills and therefore is clearly measurable. The specific accommodations and adaptations needed by the student to ensure success are stated as conditions. For example, a student's

IEP objective may specify that given three different signature labels, he will read all three, identify his name, peel off this label, and apply it on a bold line that has been drawn on his paper for 15 consecutive assignments that are turned in. Not only are the accommodations clear (e.g., three different signature labels and a bold line on his papers), but so are the specific skills involved and a criterion that is clearly measurable. Furthermore, the intent of teaching name recognition and writing by affixing the appropriate label to papers has obvious value for his adult life. Signing one's name is definitely a lifelong skill. Of critical importance, of course, is to ensure that the IEP goals and objectives written for the student in the area of literacy (as well as other areas) reflect the wishes and aspirations of the student and family. See the right column in Table 5.2 for more examples of active IEP objectives.

Table 5.2   A Comparison of Passive Versus Active Goals and Objectives

Passive/Vague Objectives	Active Objectives
SherylAnn will be read to for a minimum of 15 minutes at least 3 times each day by educational staff.	When asked questions about a story, SherylAnn will point to pictorial/color information in the book (or additional materials) to respond correctly to a minimum of 3 questions for 6 stories read.
Trevor will listen to a story for at least 5 minutes for 5 consecutive stories.	After listening to a story, Trevor will use 3 pictorial and numbered cards to correctly sequence a part of the story for 5 stories.
Jason will be positioned so as to allow him to express his thoughts on paper.	After being properly positioned, Jason will choose at least 3 tactile items related to experiences he has had to put on his journal pages once a day for 10 consecutive days.
For the entire school year, Anel will be exposed to at least 30 minutes a day of literacy experiences.	When asked a comprehension question with 2 pictorial/written options, Anel will choose the correct answer at least once every reading lesson for 10 lessons.
Danielle will participate in daily spelling lessons, as measured by teacher observation.	During spelling activities, Danielle will use her touch switch and rotary scanner to find the beginning letter (from 5 options) of at least 6 spelling words per lesson, which a peer then spells for 10 lessons.

Standard-Linked IEP Objectives

In addition to clearly stating that students are actively engaged in learning, IEP goals and objectives should also be linked to state standards in literacy. Stating what students with significant disabilities are expected to learn in regard to state standards raises expectations for these students to learn (Wehmeyer, Lattin, Lapp-Rincker, & Agran, 2003). Obviously, state standards in literacy must be interpreted in a broad manner to allow for the inclusion of students with significant disabilities. However, they must not be interpreted so broadly that it is difficult to relate expectations back to the standard. Examples of IEP objectives for different students that show the relationship to state standards in literacy can be found in Table 5.3.

| Table 5.3 | Linking Core Literacy Standards to IEP Objectives |

Core Literacy Standard	Related IEP Objective
Write for a variety of purposes and audiences, developing fluency, style, and voice	At the end of each day, Cole will write a letter to his parents by selecting the appropriate picture/ word from 2 different options and filling in at least 4 blanks in prewritten sentences that describe his day for 2 weeks.
Gather information using reference material, graphics, and electronic media	Given labeled pictures of different items, Donovan will use a picture dictionary to find a similar item, when assisted to the correct page of the dictionary, for 12 of 15 words.
Identify major themes in a story or nonfiction text	After stories have been read to Ronnie, with the accompanying objects shown and discussed, he will choose the most appropriate object or part of object representing the story from a field of 3 options for 10 of 12 consecutive stories.
Write an essay	Using photographs taken of weekend activities and a number line, Shari will correctly sequence at least 3 photographs to write about an activity for 9 of 10 such activities.

PROCEDURES FOR MEASURING STUDENT PROGRESS

Under the Individuals with Disabilities Education Act (IDEA), schools are accountable for ensuring student progress. As a result, teachers are responsible for documenting student achievement through careful measurement procedures. Unfortunately, given the many time-consuming responsibilities of teachers, some of which include preparation, teaching, adapting materials, and parent conferencing, finding time to regularly collect data becomes a challenge. Certainly, the process of collecting the data must be made as simple and straightforward as possible so that it is easy for a number of people to collect.

Data Collection

To support efficient means of measuring progress, a few aspects should be considered. As stated earlier, being clear as to what is to be used as evidence of improvement is important. Knowing exactly what the student is to demonstrate will help determine what a reasonable and meaningful criterion might be. IEP team members will need to give careful thought to what skill(s) the student will master and what will determine mastery. This information should be clearly reflected in high-quality objectives for the student.

Given the hectic schedules that most teachers experience, obtaining information on a regular basis must be efficient. Data collection must be worked into the daily schedule so that it is not overlooked. Raver (2004) stresses the importance of collecting data to measure the progress of young children with special needs and suggests that teachers may be more apt to do so if data collection is embedded in typical routines and activities. Data collection forms must be easily accessible so that they can quickly be used to gather the necessary information without a lot of difficulty. Keeping these with other materials that a student is using for a given class or activity may help facilitate their use.

Collecting data on every attempt made by every student on a daily basis may not be the most time-efficient approach. Rather, collecting certain data once a week may be more practical and sufficient. The rate of data collection will be determined by the learning rate of the student. Less frequent data collection may be sufficient for skills that are very challenging for the student and will take considerable rehearsal time to learn. A routine needs to be established for all students on a teacher's caseload, so that it is clear what data will be collected for what students and on what specific days. Scheduling data collection so that it does not all have to be completed on a given day for all objectives for all students may ease this task.

Determining who will assist in the data collection procedure may help alleviate the workload and responsibility from just one person (typically the teacher). All team members can and should assist with collecting data on student progress (Kleinert & Kearns, 2004). Such an approach makes sense when IEP goals and objectives are written collaboratively across discipline areas instead of being discipline specific (e.g., occupational therapy goals or speech goals). Different team members can be delegated responsibility for collecting data, based on when they work with a given student. When data collection forms are kept with the student, each team member can quickly determine past progress made and collect new data as indicated. Training team members to work in this collaborative and cooperative fashion will be necessary to ensure accurate and consistent data collection. Otherwise, what one team member perceives as independent performance by a student may not be seen as independent by another. To be useful, data must be accurate.

Easy-to-Use Forms

Data collection forms are based on the IEP goals and objectives for an individual student. Therefore writing clear goals and objectives with a meaningful criterion for mastery will greatly facilitate the development of appropriate data collection forms. At the very least, data forms need to collect the necessary data to show progress being made toward individual goals and objectives. However, these forms also can collect data that go beyond the immediate requirements of goals and objectives and provide educational staff with additional information about how the student learns and under what conditions. Data sheets also can contain instructional prompting strategies to serve as ongoing reminders to different team members working with a given student. In Table 5.4, a sample data collection form is shown for a third-grade student, Joshua, who is learning to identify meaningful words in his schedule. The data sheet is designed to simply tally the times he accurately and independently points to the correct word as it occurs naturally throughout each day. Instructional prompting strategies are provided to ensure that everyone working with Joshua uses a similar approach so as not to confuse him.

For some students, documenting a series of skills that reflect the understanding of basic literacy may be the target. For example, we may want to know whether a student can choose a book, orient it, open it to the first page, turn pages, and, in general, engage in a number of small skills that demonstrate what he or she knows about handling reading material. In such a case, data sheets may show a task analysis of the targeted skills, as in Table 5.5. Data are collected on each skill as it naturally occurs, with prompting strategies provided per skill.

Table 5.4   Sample Data Collection Sheet for Words on Schedule

Student: _____

Objective: Using his pictorial/written daily schedule, Joshua will point to the correct word that indicates the appropriate activity when asked to find a specific word from 3 options for 8 of 10 words daily for 2 weeks.

Schedule Words	Date 3/16	Date	Date	Date	Date	Intervention for All Words
PE	+					*Ask him to find the word(s)
Lunch						*Wait 3 seconds
Music						*Ask again and move finger toward words to guide his attention
Reading						*Wait 3 seconds
Math						*Give him flash card with word(s) on it and ask him to find the same word(s) in his schedule
Art	+					*Wait 3 seconds
Science	+					*Correct, if need be
Home	+					*Model this and say the word(s)
Go						*Praise all efforts
Time						
To						
Eat	+					

Put a + each time Joshua correctly identifies the desired word

Put a − each time Joshua requires prompting or makes a mistake

A task analysis approach to documenting progress on targeted literacy skills also applies to the skill of writing one's name on papers to be turned in. For a student with severe and multiple disabilities, assigning his name to a paper will require several subskills. The student may need an adaptation to add his name to his work, such as the use of a signature stamp or sticky prewritten labels. Instead of just documenting the physical act of using the labels or stamp, the teacher should verify the student's ability to

Table 5.5   Task Analysis of Handling a Book Used as a Data Sheet

Student: _____

Objective: When positioned in the reading area of the library or classroom, Clare will pick a book to read, orient it appropriately, open the book, turn each page and briefly attend to each page in book, and close book when finished 10 of 15 opportunities to do this.

Skills	Trial 1	Trial 2	Trial 3	Trial 4	Trial 5	Prompting Strategy
Get book	+					*Model choosing a book *Position her close to bookshelves *Ask her to choose a book *Wait 5 seconds *Pull out 3 books that will be easy to grasp and ask again *Wait 5 seconds *Support at elbow to help her reach
Orient book	–					*After she grasps the book, wait 10 seconds for her to orient book *Ask her if the book looks right and wait 5 seconds *Start to turn book, then stop *Ask again if book looks right
Open to first page	+					*After book is in correct orientation, wait 10 seconds for her to open to first page *Sit next to her and model going to first page with your book—wait 10 seconds *Start to open book
Turn pages 1 at a time	–					*Model reading by turning pages in your book—wait 10 seconds *Tap page and wait again *Start to turn first page, then stop *Correct her if she turns several pages at once (block this)
Look at each page	–					*Model reading book by looking at each page *Ask her questions about each page *Tap pages near illustrations to draw her attention *Prevent her from just flipping through the pages (block this)
Close book	+					*Model closing your book *Wait 5 seconds *Start to close her book

Key
+ = independent performance
– = not independent, needed several prompts

recognize his name first and then engage in the procedure of adding his name to the paper. Based on the student's abilities and disabilities, the number and sequence of steps involved in this task will vary. For example, grasping the signature stamp may prove to be quite challenging for a student with a physical disability, while much less so for a student with severe autism. Table 5.6 provides a data collection form for signing one's name, showing the sequence of skills needed for a particular student.

By using a task analysis approach to collect data, the smaller steps comprising the task can be delineated so that the educational staff can better determine where the student is having difficulty. The focus of instruction can then focus on the difficult steps for a given student instead of the entire sequence of skills. For instance, a student may easily recognize his name on the sticky label offered but may have considerable difficulty peeling it off and affixing it to the appropriate spot on the page. More attention can be directed to this aspect of the task, or a different accommodation (e.g., signature stamp) may be used.

Different literacy skills may require different data collection forms. If the focus of the literacy instruction is on comprehension of material, then the data collection form used to measure student progress on this particular aspect of literacy should reflect this intent. Table 5.7 provides an example of a data collection sheet used to assess a student's understanding of material read to her using pictorial options. Space on the form is provided to capture the types of questions asked of her, the number and types of pictorial options provided to her, and whether she was correct in her first attempts. Knowing what kinds of questions are asked provides the teacher with specific information concerning the student's level of understanding (e.g., responding to a simple "what" question versus a more conceptually difficult "why" or "how" question). The number and type of options provided to the student give the teacher information regarding whether or not to increase the difficulty level (e.g., two very simple and diverse options provided versus four options that are much more similar). As a result, the information gathered for this particular IEP objective not only reflects the demands of the objective but also provides guidance for future literacy instruction.

Portfolio Assessment

The use of individual portfolios to document student progress has been strongly recommended for students with disabilities, especially those with severe disabilities (Kleinert, Haigh, Kearns, & Kennedy, 2000; Kleinert & Kearns, 1999; Siegel-Causey & Allinder, 1998). Portfolios contain work samples that are representative of student achievement at different points in time. In the area of literacy work, samples might include

Table 5.6   Task Analysis Data Sheet of Signing One's Name

Student: _____

Objective: When students are told to sign their names to their papers, Edmundo will find his name stamp from 3 options, stamp it in the inkpad, and apply it to the line on his paper in 8 of 10 consecutive opportunities to do so.

Skills Sequence	Trial 1	Trial 2	Trial 3	Trial 4	Trial 5	Prompting Sequence (Praise All Attempts)
Point to or touch name on stamp	–					*Place 3 signature stamps on front of Edmundo and wait 5 seconds *Remind him what the teacher said and wait 5 seconds *Point to each stamp in turn and ask him if it's his *Correct him if he chooses the wrong one *Move correct stamp a little closer to him *Point to the first letter on all names
Grasp correct signature stamp	+					*After he has the right stamp, wait 5 seconds for him to grasp handle *Touch the stamp handle against his palm
Put stamp on inkpad	–					*Make sure inkpad is within his reach and wait 5 seconds *Tap inkpad and wait again *Ask him what he needs on his stamp and wait *Move inkpad very close *Start to manipulate stamp into inkpad
Move signature stamp to line on paper	–					*Wait 5 seconds after stamp has been put in inkpad *Ask him where his name goes *Wait 5 seconds *Point to area near line on paper and wait *Ask again and wait 5 seconds *Tap on line *Guide at elbow to line
Press stamp right above line with enough force to be legible	···					*Praise a firm press-down on the stamp *Remind him to press hard and model with another stamp *Ask him whether he thinks the imprint is readable

Key

+ = independent performance

– = not independent, needed several prompts

Table 5.7   Sample Data Sheet

IEP Objective: After being read a story or information on a topic and asked simple questions, Brandi will reach for the correct answer from a choice of 2 pictorial options for 2 of 3 questions asked per story/topic for 10 such opportunities.

Date: _____   Story/Topic: _____

Questions Asked	Options	Correct	Incorrect
1.			
2.			
3.			

Date: _____   Story/Topic: _____

Questions Asked	Options	Correct	Incorrect
1.			
2.			
3.			

Date: _____   Story/Topic: _____

Questions Asked	Options	Correct	Incorrect
1.			
2.			
3.			

samples of the student's signature, a sample schedule the student reads, and a sample story written with photographs. Samples of this nature are dated with written explanations of how they were created or used by the student. Such authentic assessment information provides a clear and accurate portrayal of a student's abilities. Over time, samples of similar skills can clearly show the progress that a student is making.

As much as possible, students with severe disabilities should be participating in the selection process of what samples are included in the portfolio. Students can be offered choices of different work samples and asked to select which sample they would prefer. Encouraging students to select samples of their work for their portfolios helps them develop important self-determination skills that will be beneficial throughout their lives.

Videotape or digital video recordings can be of considerable value to a student's portfolio (Bennett & Davis, 2001; Siegel-Causey & Allinder, 1998; Snell, 2002). Video or digital recordings can capture a student's actual ability to handle reading and writing material, how the student shares these experiences with others, the length of time a student remains actively engaged in literacy activities, and the requisite support. A video can show how a student responds to questions asked about a book or how a student writes by sequencing pictures. Such information can be taken at specified intervals during the school year to inform current team members as well as future team members new to this student. A written explanation of what the viewer is watching should accompany such recordings, with the dates of each recorded segment. In addition, videotape or digital recordings of the student provide invaluable information to family members who may or may not see similar skills at home. Seeing skills displayed by the child may help family members better articulate future goals (Bennett & Davis, 2001).

USING DATA FOR INSTRUCTIONAL PURPOSES

The regular and ongoing collection of meaningful data not only measures student progress toward individualized goals and objectives but also provides critical information on instructional programs (Halle, Chadsey, Lee, & Renzaglia, 2004; Kleinert & Kearns, 2004). If IEP goals and objectives are well written, meaningful, and reflect state curricular standards and the student is not progressing as expected, the educational team must reconsider strategies used. Lack of progress should not reflect negatively on the student, but should indicate a need to examine the program and how it is being implemented.

The effectiveness of the program can be influenced by several factors. The program may have merit but is being poorly implemented. Team members working directly with the student may not all be skilled at following the intervention procedures. Inconsistency in implementing a program across direct service providers can lead to lack of student progress. Ensuring that all team members feel comfortable and are competent implementing the agreed-upon program is essential. Team members will need to spend time discussing how the program is going, challenges that they are facing, and ways of addressing these challenges. Monitoring the consistency of program implementation over time is essential.

The program may not provide sufficient support for a student. Prompts may be ineffective. For instance, a student is to identify the first letter of his name when he signs his paperwork. He is offered the correct letter and a distracter (incorrect letter) and asked to find the first letter in his name. He randomly selects (often without looking) and is correct, on the average, 50% of the time. He does not yet recognize letters and needs more than the choice of two letters to learn this skill. Fading strategies may have been employed too soon, and increased support strategies and prompts that clarify the task for the student need to be reinstated.

Lack of reinforcement or too-limited reinforcement may be the reason why the program has limited impact. Ideally, we would hope that the natural reinforcement of learning the task (e.g., reading the book, recognizing the pictures, signing one's name) would be sufficient in strength to maintain the desired behavior. Unfortunately, with students having the most severe and multiple types of disabilities, natural consequences of this nature may be insufficient. An additional consequence that is reinforcing to a given student may have to be added to the task, and contingent on the learning of targeted skills. For instance, once a student responds correctly to simple comprehension questions asked following the reading and studying of a story or other material by choosing the appropriate pictorial representation, the student may then earn a chosen reinforcer of spending time on the computer or listening to a favorite book. Relating the reinforcer (a desired activity) to literacy further strengthens the focus on literacy learning. However, some students may need a reinforcer that is unrelated to literacy activities (e.g., being held, tickled, played with). Determining the most effective reinforcer for a student with significant disabilities is an important aspect of any instructional approach and should be given the careful consideration it deserves. Strategies have been investigated that demonstrate the ability to determine the preferences of individual students having the most profound disabilities (Alberto, Fredrick, Heflin, & Heller, 2002; Sigafoos & Mirenda, 2002). Keeping the student motivated to learn by recognizing and rewarding desired behavior is certainly a desired characteristic of any quality instructional program.

DETERMINING NEXT STEPS

Once students have demonstrated progress and met IEP goals and objectives, they will need to be challenged to continue to develop in the area of literacy. Although students may be demonstrating a certain skill level that allows them to be independent or somewhat independent, they also have a right to be challenged to learn more. Educational team members cannot be satisfied with one level of progress, but must continuously strive to help the student reach new goals in the learning process.

Review Literacy Goals

To determine the next learning objectives in literacy for a student, it is recommended that original literacy goals be reviewed. Priorities of the student and family may have changed. For example, a family may decide that printing letters is no longer appropriate for their daughter, age 15, who has been struggling with this skill for many years. Instead, they feel it would be more useful for her if she could express herself using the word/pictorial icons on specialized software (e.g., IntelliTalk II and Overlay Maker from IntelliTools).

Some goals may not have been attained by the student, yet are still considered important by the family and educational team. The student may have attained partial steps of the desired goal but may not have mastered all aspects of the goals. For example, one goal for a student involved having him choose a book or magazine, orient it, begin at the front of the book, and turn each page, looking at the pictorial/written information on each page. The student, Jake, chooses reading material and orients it correctly; however, he flips through it rapidly, turning several pages at once. He typically looks at only one page. His family and teachers still feel that he could get more enjoyment out of a book if he could go through it more slowly and systematically. Therefore the goal will be maintained, and the focus of intervention will address Jake's need to slow down, turn individual pages in a book, and look at the individual pages. Obviously, determining the next steps to take is a highly individualized decision resting upon a number of unique variables. The educational team will need to consider the age of the student, interest level, physical and cognitive abilities, rate of progress made, and literacy demands of the environment to arrive at the appropriate next steps for the student.

Raise Expectations

As students demonstrate progress on IEP goals and objectives, the education team can work together to expand the student's literacy skills. Helping the student reach greater independence in literacy activities as well as broadening understanding and ability to express oneself clearly should be goals. Referring to state standards that remain unmet may help focus the team on possible goals.

What Are the Logical Next Steps?

Methods of gradually increasing the difficulty of the literacy task attempted should be considered. The amount of literacy information can be increased (e.g., longer pictorial/word sentences read versus one picture/word). The complexity and difficulty of the type of comprehension questions asked can be increased (e.g., not just "what" or "who" questions, but "how" and "why"). The number of potential answers for comprehension questions can be increased from two to three or four. The type of symbols used by the student can be made increasingly more abstract. For example, a student has learned to make use of objects and parts of objects in her receptive and expressive communication as well as her reading of these items. Since this student has vision, it makes sense to teach her to recognize pictorial information. Photographs of the objects/parts of object she uses can be paired with these items until the items can be gradually faded. Recognizing pictorial representation of items is a more abstract level of understanding and will represent definite progress for this student. In addition, using photographs and other pictorial information rather than objects will make it much easier for the team when adapting the curriculum and creating literacy materials. Students also can be encouraged to access a wider variety of literacy materials (e.g., not just magazines on one topic). Of course, accessing a broader range of topics will depend on the student's interests and on the support available to ensure that the student has the opportunity to continue to experience different events.

Next steps in writing could include progressing from selecting more than one letter stamp when writing one's name, making controlled checkmarks versus scribbling, or actively searching for the brailled sentence and accompanying item on a page versus having them brought to the student. Being able to sequence three photographs of a common event in a row to "write" a story would be a possible next step for a student able to sequence two photographs. The practical aspect of next steps should be obvious to ensure that students are working toward desired outcomes in literacy. Choosing appropriate next steps will require revisiting original desired outcomes that the family and rest of the team may have had for a student to determine whether they are still desired and attainable.

SUMMARY

This chapter has stressed the critical importance of measuring student progress and ensuring that students are learning. While a standardized approach to measurement that measures progress along a strict hierarchy of isolated skills is not recommended, other approaches show promise.

A variety of alternative assessments (e.g., interviews, observations, videotaping, a portfolio of student work) have been shown to adequately document student learning (Browder, Spooner, Algozzine, et al., 2003; Kleinert & Kearns, 2004; Siegel-Causey & Allinder, 1998). Analyzing the student's current and anticipated learning environments should play an important role in determining what skills the student will benefit from the most.

Well-written IEP goals and objectives that are clearly measurable and relate to core standards in literacy will aid in gathering quality student progress data. This information not only ensures accurate student assessment but also reflects on the effectiveness of the intervention strategies used to teach literacy. Factors impacting the effectiveness of the program can then be analyzed to determine what modifications are needed. Careful monitoring of a student's progress as well as changes in the student's interests and desires should be used to consider what direction to continue in literacy instruction.

6 The Future for Literacy Access and Instruction

KEY CONCEPTS

- Research is still needed to determine the most effective intervention strategies for students with severe disabilities.
- Early intervention is critical to support the development of literacy skills.
- Technology has greatly advanced the field, although gaps still exist for those with the most complex disabilities.
- Training teachers and other service providers methods of literacy instruction and available technology will be critical to ensure literacy learning for students.
- The impact on a student's quality of life should be a critical factor when determining the importance of literacy instruction for students with significant disabilities.

The most optimistic aspect of having limited research in the field of literacy for students with very limited communication skills is that there is so much more to learn. We don't know exactly what these students can learn, and we have not researched the most efficient ways to teach them. Much work needs to be done, and the results of that labor will benefit teachers and students alike.

IMPROVED STRATEGIES TO SUPPORT LITERACY GOALS

Due to the limited research in the area of literacy instruction for students with the most significant disabilities, adopting a balanced approach to literacy and following recommended guidelines for teaching literacy to all students makes the most sense. However, it remains unclear what components of a balanced literacy approach are most effective for students with severe disabilities, especially since this is such a highly diverse population. For instance, what are the best strategies to use to teach basic phonetic awareness skills, and how long should such intervention be tried? How should such instruction be modified for students unable to physically produce speech? In a review of the literature for the use of phonetic analyses with students having mental retardation, Joseph and Seery (2004) found very limited research on phonetic instruction for students with mild-to-moderate disabilities, let alone those with more severe impairments. Moreover, questions remain regarding effective ways to allow students with minimal language skills to engage meaningfully in literacy activities. Bridging the experiential void for students unable to see and speak continues to present a major challenge. Without the distance sense of vision and the language skills to discuss events, effective strategies remain elusive.

Research is needed to investigate the most effective strategies to bypass the challenges that these students face of limited symbolic communication; limited access to the world due to physical, cognitive, and sensory disabilities; and difficulty understanding abstract representations. Given the population and its diverse traits, that research will probably occur on a one-by-one basis, making it difficult to generalize findings. Identifying what works and what doesn't will take a long time, which leaves teachers and parents alike to struggle without the foundation in research that would be most helpful.

STRENGTHENING EARLY INTERVENTION SERVICES

Much has been written on the importance of supporting a strong partnership between home and school (Anderson, Hiebert, Scott, & Wilkinson, 1995; Neuman, 1999; Ollila & Mayfield, 1992). The critical need for such a strong partnership is clearly evident in the area of literacy. Literacy learning begins at home as family members support language learning, build a broad experiential base, and introduce children to many basic beginning reading and writing skills (Adams, 1990; Cullingford, 2001). Perhaps most important, families have the opportunity to stress the importance of literacy and instill in children the joy of reading and writing.

Given the importance of home involvement in the development of literacy skills, strengthening this involvement by alerting families to its critical impact on future school success is recommended. Early intervention is essential for young children for whom literacy learning may on the surface appear a less critical need. These young children may present a number of physical, sensory, cognitive, and health impairments that may overshadow the need for literacy learning. Helping families recognize the importance of developing a wide experiential base for their children despite limitations faced by the children would help ensure the experiences upon which language is based. This support would need to consider family style, preferences, cultural, and religious beliefs. However, daily experiences do not have to be extraordinary and should reflect the typical activities and routines of the family. Where added support may be needed is in identifying ways for the child with the most complex disabilities to be actively involved. Families may also need support to develop the most meaningful ways to represent familiar items and activities for their children to aid this involvement. Marvin (1994) suggested that teachers will need to be trained to offer parents ideas for embedding literacy into typical routines as well as what they can expect to see from their children during these activities.

Effective communication intervention for the youngest children with severe and multiple disabilities will continue to require our field's attention. Encouraging ongoing communication from interactions with the youngest child would help that child in the acquisition of language and with the recognition that people, items, and actions have names that are the building blocks for later literacy learning. Such intervention requires a creative and highly individualized approach to make communication meaningful for the child. Broadening early intervention services to include foundational literacy learning and providing family members with the skills and materials to make this happen are critical goals for our field.

FUTURE ADVANCES IN TECHNOLOGY

The age of technology has greatly advanced our ability to support the literacy learning of all students (Koppenhaver & Erickson, 1998). Furthermore, specific attention is being paid to those students for whom the use of technology is challenging. New software on the market contains interesting sound effects and entrancing use of graphics, color, and movement and allows easy access through scanning and switch use. Alternate keyboards and switches with switch interface to the computer are becoming even easier to use and to program. Touch-free access to manipulating software programs such as the Cyberlink and Magentec, where the control for the cursor is worn on the forehead, can open doors to students unable to control arm and hand movements. The interface between user and computer will continue to improve so that minimal physical and cognitive effort will be needed. It may not be that far in the future when we will be able to interface a user's thoughts and feelings to the computer without much concentrated effort on the user's part. This potential use of computers for students who have struggled for so long to make their thoughts known to others is extremely exciting.

Future research in the area of technology is needed to help determine how graphic (and other) symbols on augmentative communication devices influence literacy learning. Are certain symbols more appropriate than others? What are the best symbols to use for students who have no functional vision and have severe cognitive disabilities? Increased attention still needs to be paid to the development of assistive technology that will be of assistance to those students who do not use vision and have limited language skills. Individuals who are deaf-blind and are learning basic interaction skills fall under this category.

Initial research has identified the potentially positive impact that speech-generating devices, an aspect of some augmentative communication devices, can have on the development of language (Blischak, Lombardino, & Dyson, 2003; Schlosser, 2003). More research is needed to determine the most efficient ways to make use of this finding for *all* students.

Bridging the Research-to-Practice Gap

Despite gains being made in the area of assistive technology to support the learning of students with disabilities, practitioners tend to underuse this technology, especially for students with cognitive disabilities (Wehmeyer, 1999). Students who are blind or deaf-blind and have severe cognitive impairments are at a particular disadvantage when attempting to make use of available technology (Harding, 2003; Kovach & Kenyon, 2003). As a result, those students who need the most support to access their environments may not be benefiting from progress made in this area. Teachers and related services providers need to stay abreast of the latest developments in the field of technology and learn how to bring these advancements to their students. They need to receive ongoing training in the area of technology to know what is available, how it can be most effectively used by different students, and how to teach these students the use of the technology. In addition, they will need to learn ways of helping family members attain the necessary technology for their children, which requires knowledge of the Medicare system.

IMPACT ON PERSONNEL PREPARATION

To ensure that all students receive and benefit from literacy instruction, teachers will need training in this area. Outdated ideas that students must obtain certain IQ scores or scores from developmental checklists or reach prescribed developmental milestones must be eschewed in favor of the belief that all students are entitled to solid literacy instruction. Equally outdated beliefs in the need to separate students on the basis of ability to ensure learning for everyone must be replaced with the knowledge of the benefits of inclusive education for all students (see Ryndak & Fisher, 2003). When students with the most challenging disabilities are educated in general education classrooms, the opportunities for literacy instruction are obvious (Browder & Spooner, 2003; Davern, Schnorr, & Black, 2003).

Expectations for achievement in inclusive environments are higher, and the advantages of teachers working together to support all students become literate members of their society are evident. For example, a study by White, Garrett, Kearns, and Grisham-Brown (2003) focused on alternate assessment results in three states for 24 students labeled deaf-blind. Findings from this study indicated that when students had more time to interact with peers with no disabilities, their communication skills improved and they scored higher than those without this opportunity on alternate assessments. Personnel preparation programs must ensure that the values of inclusive education and high expectations for all students are presented to teachers in training—both general and special education.

Impact on Quality of Life

Research is needed to identify the impact that enhanced literacy learning will have on a student's quality of life. Although a sound assumption, little, if any, research exists as verification. What does literacy actually mean to students having the most significant disabilities? Is the quality of their lives actually better as a result? Is there a difference between students with severe disabilities who do and do not have ongoing access to literacy events? What factors can be analyzed to determine the answer to these questions? There is much we do not yet know, which provides ample reason to pursue the answers. However, waiting for these answers to emerge is not what is being recommended.

We know that some students progress from using primarily pictorial information to recognizing words and understanding the message contained within those words. Such progress indicates greater independence and a reduced need to depend on others for direction. With this skill, students can follow pictorial/written directions that may enable them to obtain a job and learn the tasks of that job without excessive external support. Thus literacy learning clearly supports the transition from school to adult life, which is one obvious goal of a quality education. Students who learn to recognize the symbolic representation of options in their environments can make choices that reflect their preferences. This choice-making skill, in turn, leads to the formation of self-determination, which gives the student newfound levels of control.

Students once unable to sit comfortably next to someone during a literacy activity are now able to request that a story be read and seem to enjoy the time spent in close proximity with another person engaged in the same activity. This social closeness enhances the prospects of future social interactions and of the recognition that other people can be very reinforcing.

A few students known to the author have progressed from not recognizing what a picture was (e.g., using it to flap in the air or put in their mouth) to having preferences for certain stories, holding a book, orienting it correctly, and turning pages to look at favorite pages. By learning these series of skills, these students, whether they ever learn more conventional literacy skills or not, have learned to entertain themselves in a very appropriate manner. Thus, a lifelong skill that can be used anywhere has been learned. In addition to self-entertainment, these students may be gaining important information from the books they are reading. Further research is needed to determine how much information students with significant disabilities can obtain from interactions with literacy materials without direct instruction.

All of the examples of progress provided above impact a student's quality of life. Outcomes of literacy instruction at any level can have profound effects on all aspects of a student's life. Therefore fears that a particular student may be too disabled to benefit from instruction in literacy should be dismissed. The least dangerous assumption would be to assume that literacy is meaningful to individuals with significant disabilities and that by ensuring access to literacy activities and quality instruction, we can continue to search for the answers to important questions without depriving any group of students of important educational opportunities.

Resources

www.aacintervention.com/talk.htm

This Web site provides information on augmentative and alternative communication products as well as activities related to intervention. Information is provided with regard to creating literacy-based communication boards. Literacy sources are provided as well as presentations being offered and links to other related sites.

AAC Literacy Project
Callier Center/University of Texas at Dallas
www.ACT.utdallas.edu

This project is a resource for parents and teachers interested in facilitating literacy skills in children who use augmentative and alternative communication.

Bloom, Y., & Bhargava, D. (2003). *Let's read together. Parts 1 & 2: Using commercially available books to promote literacy.* Beecroft, Australia: Innovative Programming Options.
bloom@tig.com.au
61-2-9876 3568
www.innovativeprogramming.net.au

This package of materials (manual and CD) provides many creative ways of making reading accessible for students who are not verbal and communicate via alternative modes. Materials are specifically designed for working with students who have multiple sensory impairments.

Bookshare.org
www.bookshare.org

This Web site provides numerous titles of books that can be downloaded. Universal design for achieving literacy is the premise, with digitalized text and voice output available for students who need to listen to books read. Copies can be obtained in braille versions as needed.

Center for Literacy and Disability Studies (CLDS)
CB #7335, TR #48, UNC-CH
Chapel Hill, NC 27599-7335
www.med.unc.edu/ahs/dds
Dr. Karen Erickson
919-966-8828

CLDS promotes literacy learning and use for individuals of all ages with disabilities. There is a stated belief in the right of all individuals to learn to read and write. The center helps develop research-based strategies, tools, and curricula in literacy. Trainings are provided to families and professionals. There are links to other literacy sites as well as resources, projects, and trainings provided.

CLAS Institute (Culturally and Linguistically Appropriate Services Early Childhood Research Institute)
http://clas.uiuc.edu

CLAS has more than 2,000 materials on various subjects, including several disabilities and emergent literacy. Summaries of materials are provided as well as intended audiences and the available format (video, audiotape, print, poster).

Clicker 4 and Clicker Animations
Crick Software, Inc.
50 116th Ave SE
Suite 211
Bellevue, WA 98004
866-332-7425
www.cricksoft.com

Clicker is a supportive writing tool with a graphic library of more than 1,000 pictures. Custom-made pictures can be easily imported to personalize work. Clicker animations add movement to the graphics that support the written text.

Greenhouse Publications
Interactive Reading Books
P.O. Box 802742
Santa Clarita, CA 91380-2742
661-263-7661
joangreen2000@aol.com

Interactive Reading Books are designed to help children associate pictures with words. Children actively engage in reading and writing the books by moving Velcro-backed, colorful pictures into a particular sequence. Children match, label, identify, and sequence pictures to create sentences.

IntelliTools Reading: Balanced Literacy
1720 Corporate Circle
Petaluma, CA 94954-6924
800-899-6687
lray@intellitools.com
www.intellitools.com

Balanced Literacy is a theme-based, balanced approach to literacy incorporating, guided reading, self-selected reading, explicit phonics, and writing-skill units. This program is research based and accessible.

Kelly, J., & Friend, T. (1993). *Hands-on reading.* Solana Beach, CA: Mayer-Johnson.

This book provides examples of many different reading activities for students with severe disabilities, especially those using augmentative communication devices.

Kelly, J., & Friend, T. (1995). *More hands-on reading.* Solana Beach, CA: Mayer-Johnson.

This later edition adds to the examples of active learning opportunities to help support literacy learning for students with severe disabilities.

Kuster, J. M. (2003). Picture it! Free art for therapy materials. Retrieved from http://www.mnsu.edu/dept/comdis/kuster4/part49.html, September 11, 2003.

This Web site article offers practical suggestions for locating free graphic art to use in the development of literacy materials. Numerous Web sites with specific information of how to download are provided for teachers and family members to access.

Mayer-Johnson Co.
P.O. Box 1579
Solana Beach, CA 92075
800-588-4548
www.mayer-johnson.com

This company offers tips, tutorials and materials to share. Research on assistive technology is available. Many different products are advertised that support literacy learning at many different levels of ability, such as Writing with Symbols 2000 and Speaking Dynamically Pro with Boardmaker symbols.

Mervine, P., Mark, M., & Burton, M. (1995). *I can cook, too!* Solana Beach, CA: Mayer-Johnson.
This book is full of recipes using pictorial symbols from Mayer-Johnson.

Musselwhite, C. R. (1993). *RAPS: Reading activities project for older students.* Phoenix, AZ: Southwest Human Development.
RAPS specifically targets literacy activities for the older student who has severe disabilities.

Musselwhite, C., & King De-Baun, P. (1997). *Emerging literacy success: Merging whole language and technology for students with disabilities.* Park City, UT: Creative Communicating.
This book provides a number of creative activities for emergent literacy learners of all ages.

News-2-You
P.O. Box 550
Huron, OH 44839
800-697-6575
djclark@sprintmail.com
www.news-2-you.com
News-2-You is a symbol-based newspaper for students who need graphic support to read. This can be downloaded from the Internet weekly and contains the latest current events, jokes, activity pages, and a great deal more to make it a very useful educational tool.

Quill, K. A. (2000). *Do, watch, listen, say.* Baltimore: Paul H. Brookes.
This book gives excellent strategies for working with children having autism. It targets the need to provide visual information as well as other modes of input to support learning.

Tack-Tiles Braille Systems
P.O. Box 475
Plaistow, NH 03865
800-822-5845
Braille@tack-tiles.com
www.tack-tiles.com
Tack-Tiles are Lego sets with raised braille dots on the top surface of each piece to represent the alphabet and various contractions inherent in the system. The large, durable surface may make it a useful adaptation for students with multiple disabilities who are learning braille.

The Thinking Reader Project
CAST
Universal Design for Learning
39 Cross Street
Peabody, MA 01960
978-531-8555
rmcadow@cast.org
www.cast.org/udl/index

The Thinking Reader Project is an interactive digital learning environment to support the development of beginning reading skills and comprehension strategies for students with intellectual impairments.

UKanDu Little Books
Don Johnston Incorporated
26799 W. Commerce Dr.
Volo, IL 60073
800-999-4660
www.donjohnston.com

Designed for young readers, this switch-activated software allows students to create their own stories and learn beginning literacy skills.

Glossary

Alternative assessment—a process of obtaining information on an individual's progress without using standardized forms or procedures. Alternative assessment typically involves observation, checklists, and portfolio assessment.

Assistive technology—any item or piece of equipment (commercial or handmade) that is used to increase, maintain, or improve the functional capabilities of individuals with disabilities. This also includes any service that assists the individual with disabilities in the selection, acquisition, or use of assistive technology.

Augmentative and alternative communication—a system of communication supports and services for individuals who do not rely on speech for the majority of their communicative interactions.

Braille—a tactile system of reading and writing for individuals who are blind. This system of embossed characters formed by using combinations of six dots, consisting of two vertical columns of three dots each, provides a means of reading and writing through the sense of touch.

Collaborative teaming—the process by which all team members work cooperatively together to meet the needs of individual students.

Core curriculum—standard grade-level curriculum typically covering areas of language arts, mathematics, science, and social studies.

Ecological inventories—an alternative assessment process that is observational in nature and delineates the skill demands of different environments (ecologies) for individuals.

Emergent literacy—initial skills in literacy that signal understanding related to literacy, such as proper orientation of reading materials, turning pages to find more information, identifying pictorial information, and understanding that print has meaning.

Facilitated communication—alternative means of expression for a person who cannot speak or whose speech is highly limited and who cannot point reliably. Method used to communicate for individuals having severe disabilities.

Individuals With Disabilities Education Act (IDEA)—1997 reauthorization of the federal law to provide education and related services to all children and youth with disabilities mandates that each student receive a free appropriate public education in the least restrictive environment.

Integrative service delivery—related services professionals provide services and supports within the general education environment to facilitate student learning within ongoing activities.

Joint attention—an early-developing social communicative skill in which two individuals mutually focus on the same object, event, or person.

Mutual tactile attention—joint attention and sharing an activity or object through noncontrolling mutual touch.

No Child Left Behind (NCLB)—2001 federal law designed to ensure accountability in the schools with set standards in reading, mathematics, and other subjects.

Page fluffers—handmade adaptations that affix to pages to separate them, making it easier to turn pages and bypassing the need for fine motor control of the fingers.

Person-centered planning—an individualized and personal approach to supporting a person's plan for the future. Significant people in the person's life play supportive roles, and an action plan is the result of listening to the person's dreams.

Personnel preparation—the process of teaching professionals and paraprofessionals to acquire the skills and knowledge needed in the educational system.

Portfolio assessment—a form of alternative assessment that is highly individualized and reflects the progress of individual students through selection of representative samples of work (e.g., written sample of a book report, videotaped lesson of a task being performed, math homework sheet).

Positioning—the support of an individual with severe physical disabilities into a specific position for therapeutic and functional reasons. Support can be provided by an individual or by equipment designed to maintain the individual in a given position.

Speech-generating device—an augmentative communication device that produces speech as part of its communicative output.

Standard—curricular benchmark that indicates mastery of specific content.

Standardized assessment—norm-referenced tests that compare individual performance with the overall group tested.

Tactile strategies—the use of touch, objects, tangible symbols, and sign to convey information.

Voice output communication aid—an augmentative communication device containing messages with synthesized or digital recording of a voice that an individual would use to make needs known to others. The device also can be used to support an individual's receptive communication skills.

References

Adams, M. J. (1990). *Beginning to read: Thinking and learning about print.* Cambridge: MIT Press.

Agran, M., King-Sears, M. E., Wehmeyer, M. L., & Copeland, S. R. (2003). *Student-directed learning.* Baltimore: Paul H. Brookes.

Alberto, P. A., & Fredrick, L. D. (2000). Teaching picture reading as an enabling skill. *TEACHING Exceptional Children, 33*(1), 60–64.

Alberto, P. A., Fredrick, L. D., Heflin, L. J., & Heller, K. W. (2002). Preference variability and the instruction of choice making with students with severe intellectual disabilities. *Education and Training in Mental Retardation and Developmental Disabilities, 31*(1), 70–88.

Allington, R. L., & Baker, K. (1999). Best practices in literacy instruction for children with special needs. In S. B. Neuman, & M. Pressley (Eds.), *Best practices in literacy instruction* (pp. 292–310). New York: Guilford Press.

Anderson, R. C., Hiebert, E. H., Scott, J. A., & Wilkinson, I. A. G. (1995). *Becoming a nation of readers: The report of the commission on reading.* Washington, DC: National Institute of Education.

Barudin, S. I., & Hourcade, J. J. (1990). Relative effectiveness of three methods of reading instruction in developing specific recall and transfer skills in learners with moderate and severe mental retardation. *Education and Training in Mental Retardation, 25,* 286–298.

Bennett, D. E., & Davis, M. A. (2001). The development of an alternate assessment system for students with significant disabilities. *Diagnostique: Assessment for Effective Intervention, 26,* 15–34.

Beukelman, D., & Mirenda, P. (1998). Augmentative and alternative communication: *Management of severe communication disorders in children and adults.* Baltimore: Paul H. Brookes.

Beukelman, D., Mirenda, P., & Sturm, J. (1998). Literacy development of AAC users. In D. Beukelman & P. Mirenda (Eds.), *Augmentative and alternative communication: Management of severe communication disorders in children and adults* (pp. 355–390). Baltimore: Paul H. Brookes.

Biklen, D. (1993). *Communication unbound: How facilitated communication is challenging traditional views of autism and ability/disability.* New York: Teachers College Press.

Blackstone, S. W., & Berg, M. H. (2003). *Social networks: A communication inventory for individuals with complex communication needs and their communication partners.* Monterey, CA: Augmentive Communication.

Blischak, D. M. (1995). Thomas the writer: Case study of a child with severe physical, speech, and visual impairments. *Language, Speech, and Hearing Services, 26,* 11–20.

Blischak, D. M., Lombardino, L. J., & Dyson, A. T. (2003). Use of speech-generating devices: In support of natural speech. *Augmentative and Alternative Communication, 19,* 29–35.

Bloome, D., & Katz, L. (1997). Literacy as social practice and classroom chronotopes. *Reading & Writing Quarterly, 13,* 205–226.

Boundy, K. (2000). Including students with disabilities in standards based educational reform. *TASH Newsletter, 26*(4), 4–5, 21.

Brady, N. C., & McLean, I. K. (1996). Arbitrary symbol learning by adults with severe mental retardation: Comparison of lexigrams and printed words. *American Journal on Mental Retardation, 100,* 423–427.

Browder, D. M., Fallin, K., Davis, S., & Karvonen, M. (2003). Consideration of what may influence student outcomes on alternate assessment. *Education and Training in Developmental Disabilities, 38,* 255–270.

Browder, D. M., & Lalli, J. S. (1991). Review of research on sight word instruction. *Research in Development Disability, 12,* 203–228.

Browder, D. M., & Spooner, F. (2003). Understanding the purpose and process of alternative assessment. In D. L. Ryndak & S. Alper (Eds.), *Curriculum and instruction for students with significant disabilities in inclusive settings* (pp. 51–72). Boston: Allyn & Bacon.

Browder, D., Spooner, F., Ahlgrim-Delzell, L., Flowers, C., Algozzine, B., & Karvonen, M. (2003). A content analysis of the curricular philosophies reflected in states' alternate assessment performance indicators. *Research and Practice for Persons with Severe Disabilities, 28,* 165–181.

Browder, D. M., Spooner, F., Algozzine, R., Ahlgrim-Delzell, L. Flowers, C., & Karvonen, M. (2003). What we know and need to know about alternate assessment. *Exceptional Children, 70,* 45–61.

Browder, D. M., & Xin Yan, P. (1998). A meta-analysis and review of sight word research and its implication for teaching functional reading to individuals with moderate and severe disabilities. *Journal of Special Education, 32*(3), 130–154.

Brown, F., Gothelf, C. R., Guess, D., & Lehr, D. (1998). Self-determination for individuals with the most severe disabilities: Moving past chimera. *Journal of the Association for Persons with Severe Handicaps, 23,* 17–26.

Cardinal, D. N. (2002, May). A request to reconsider facilitated communication: Some ideas, evidence, and the presumption of competence. *TASH Connections, 28*(5), 15–16.

Carpenter, C. D., Bloom, L. A., & Boat, M. B. (1999). Guidelines for special educators: Achieving socially valid outcomes. *Intervention in School & Clinic, 34,* 143–149.

Carter, M., & Iacono, T. (2002). Professional judgments of the intentionality of communicative acts. *Augmentative and Alternative Communication, 18,* 177–191.

Chen, D., Chan, S., & Brekken, L. (2000). *Conversations for three: Communicating through interpreters* [Video & booklet]. Baltimore: Paul H. Brookes.

Clay, M. M. (1993). *An observation in survey of early literacy achievement.* Portsmouth, NH: Heinemann.

Collins, B. C., Branson, T. A., & Hall, M. (1995). Teaching generalized reading of cooking product labels to adolescents with mental disabilities through the use of key words taught by peer tutors. *Education and Training in Mental Retardation and Developmental Disabilities, 30,* 65–75.

Connors, F. A. (1992). Reading instruction for students with moderate mental retardation: Review and analysis of research. *American Journal of Mental Retardation, 103,* 1–11.

Copeland, S. R., & Hughes, C. (2000). Acquisition of a picture prompt strategy to increase independent performance. *Education and Training in Mental Retardation and Developmental Disabilities, 35,* 294–305.

Corso, R. M., Santos, R. M., Roof, V. (2002). Honoring diversity in early childhood education materials. *TEACHING Exceptional Children, 34*(3), 30–36.

Craig, S. E., Haggart, A. G., & Hull, K. M. (1999, Spring). Integrating therapies into the educational setting: Strategies for supporting children with severe disabilities. *Physical Disabilities: Education and Related Services, XVII*(2), 91–109.

Cress, C. J. (2003). Expanding children's early augmented behaviors to support symbolic development. In J. Reichle, D. R. Beukelman, & J. C. Light (Eds.), *Exemplary practices for beginning communicators: Implications for AAC* (pp. 219–272). Baltimore: Paul H. Brookes.

Cress, C. J., & Marvin, C. A. (2003). Common questions about AAC services in early intervention. *Augmentative and Alternative Communication, 19,* 254–272.

Crossley, R. (1994). *Facilitated communication training.* New York: Teachers College Press.

Cullingford, C. (2001). *How children learn to read and how to help them.* London: Kogan Page.

Cunningham, P. M. (1995). *Phonics they use: Words for reading and writing* (2nd ed.). New York: HarperCollins.

Davern, L., Schnorr, R., & Black, J. W. (2003). Planning instruction for the diverse classroom: Approaches that facilitate the inclusion of all students.

In D. L. Ryndak & S. Alper (Eds.), *Curriculum and instruction for students with significant disabilities in inclusive settings* (pp. 340–361). Boston: Allyn & Bacon.

DeTemple, J. M. (2001). Parents and children reading books together. In D. K. Dickinson & P. O. Tabors (Eds.), *Beginning literacy with language* (pp. 31–52). Baltimore: Paul H. Brookes.

Downing, J. (1988). Active vs. passive programming: A critique of IEP objectives for students with the most severe disabilities. *Journal of the Association for Persons With Severe Handicaps, 13,* 197–201.

Downing, J. E. (2002). *Including students with severe and multiple disabilities in typical classrooms: Practical strategies for teachers* (2nd ed.). Baltimore: Paul H. Brookes.

Downing, J. E. (2003). Accommodating motor and sensory impairments in inclusive settings. In D. L. Ryndak & S. Alper (Eds.), *Curriculum and instruction for students with significant disabilities in inclusive settings* (2nd ed., pp. 411–429). Boston: Allyn & Bacon.

Downing, J. E. (2004). Communication skills. In F. P. Orelove, D. Sobsey, & R. K. Silberman (Eds.), *Educating children with multiple disabilities: A collaborative approach* (4th ed., pp. 529–562). Baltimore: Paul H. Brookes.

Downing, J. E., & Chen, D. (2003). Using tactile strategies with students who are blind and have severe disabilities. *TEACHING Exceptional Children, 36*(2), 56–60.

Downing, J. E., Eichinger, J., & Williams, L. J. (1997). Inclusive education for students with severe disabilities: Comparative views of principals and educators at different levels of implementation. *Remedial and Special Education, 18,* 133–142.

Downing, J. E., & Peckham-Hardin, K. (2001). Daily schedules: A helpful learning tool. *TEACHING Exceptional Children, 33*(3), 62–68.

Downing, J. E., Spencer, S., & Cavallaro, C. (2004). The development of an inclusive charter elementary school: Lessons learned. *Research and Practice for Persons with Severe Disabilities, 29,* 11–24.

Durand, V. M., Mapstone, E., & Youngblood, L. (1999). The role of communication partners. In J. Downing (Ed.), *Teaching communication skills to students with disabilities* (pp. 139–156). Baltimore: Paul H. Brookes.

Ehri, L. C. (2000). Learning to read and learning to spell: Two sides of a coin. *Topics in Language Disorders, 20*(3), 19–36.

Elder, P. S., & Goossens, C. (1996). *Engineering training environments for interactive augmentative communication: Strategies for adolescents and adults who are moderately/severely developmentally delayed.* Birmingham, AL: Southeast Augmentative Communication Conference Publications.

Erickson, K. A., & Koppenhaver, D. A. (1995). Developing a literacy program for children with severe disabilities. *The Reading Teacher, 48,* 676–683.

Erickson, K. A., & Koppenhaver, D. A. (1998). Using the "write talk-nology" with Patrick. *TEACHING Exceptional Children, 31*(1), 58–64.

Erickson, K. A., Koppenhaver, D. A., & Yoder, D. E. (1994). *Literacy and adults with developmental disabilities.* Philadelphia: National Center on Adult Literacy.

Falvey, M. A., Blair, M., Dingle, M., & Franklin, N. (2000). Creating a community for learners with varied needs. In R. Villa & J. Thousand (Eds.), *Restructuring for a caring and effective education* (pp. 186–207). Baltimore: Paul H. Brookes.

Fewell, R. R. (2000). Assessment of young children with special needs: Foundations for tomorrow. *Topics in Early Childhood Special Education, 20,* 38–42.

Fisher, D., & Frey, N. (2004). *Improving adolescent literacy: Strategies at work.* Upper Saddle River, NJ: Merrill Prentice Hall.

Fisher, D., & Kennedy, C. H. (2001). Differentiated instruction for diverse middle school students. In C. H. Kennedy & D. Fisher (Eds.), *Inclusive middle schools* (pp. 61–72). Baltimore: Paul H. Brookes.

Fisher, D., & Ryndak, D. L. (2001). *The foundations of inclusive education: A compendium of articles on effective strategies to achieve inclusive education.* Baltimore: TASH.

Fisher, M., & Meyer, L. H. (2002). Development and social competence after two years for students enrolled in inclusive and self-contained educational programs. *Research and Practice for Persons with Severe Disabilities, 27,* 165–174.

Foley, B. (1993). The development of literacy in individuals with severe speech and motor impairments. *Topics in Language Disorders, 13*(2), 16–32.

Ford, A., Davern, L., & Schnorr, R. (2001). Learners with significant disabilities: Curriculum relevance in an era of standards-based reform. *Remedial and Special Education, 22,* 214–222.

Fossett, B., Smith V., & Mirenda, P. (2003). Facilitating oral language and literacy development during general education activities. In D. L. Ryndak & S. Alper (Eds.), *Curriculum and instruction for students with significant disabilities in inclusive settings* (pp. 173–205). Boston: Allyn & Bacon.

Freeman, S. F. N., & Alkin, M. C. (2000). Academic and social attainments of children with mental retardation in general education and special education settings. *Remedial and Special Education, 21*(1), 3–18.

French, N. K. (2003). Paraeducators in special education programs. *Focus on Exceptional Children, 36*(2), 1–16.

Gallego, M. A., & Hollingsworth, S. (2000). *What counts as literacy: Challenging the classroom standard.* New York: Teachers College Press.

Gambrell, L. B., & Mazzoni, S. A. (1999). Principals of best practice: Finding the common ground. In L. B. Gambrell, L. M. Morrow, S. B. Newman, & M. Pressley (Eds.), *Best practices in literacy instruction* (pp. 11–21). New York: Guilford Press.

Gately, S. (2004). Developing concept of word: The work of emergent readers. *TEACHING Exceptional Children, 36*(6), 16–22.

Giangreco, M. F., Cloninger, C. J., & Iverson, V. S. (1998). *Choosing outcomes and accommodations for children (COACH): A guide to educational planning for students with disabilities* (2nd ed.). Baltimore: Paul H. Brookes.

Giangreco, M. F., Edelman, S., & Dennis, R. (1991). Common professional practices that interfere with the integrated delivery of related services. *Remedial and Special Education, 12*(2), 16–24.

Giangreco, M. F., Edelman, S. W., Luiselli, T. E., & MacFarland, S. Z. (1996). Supported service decision making for students with multiple service needs: Evaluative data. *Journal of the Association for Persons with Severe Handicaps, 21,* 135–144.

Giangreco, M. F., Edelman, S. W., Luiselli, T. E., & MacFarland, S. Z. (1997). Helping or hovering? Effects of instructional assistant proximity on students with disabilities. *Exceptional Children, 64,* 7–18.

Giangreco, M. F., Edelman, S. W., Nelson, C., Young, M. R., & Kiefer-O'Donnell, R. (1999). Changes in educational team membership for students who are deaf-blind in general education classes. *Journal of Visual Impairments and Blindness, 93,* 166–173.

Goals 2000: Educate America Act. (1994). Pub. L. 103–227, 20 U.S.C. 5801 et seq.

Goddard, P. (2002, June). It's your move. *TASH Connections, 28*(6), 10–11.

Gordon Pershey, M., & Gilbert, T. W. (2002). Christine: A case study of literacy acquisition by an adult with development disability. *Mental Retardation, 40,* 219–234.

Green, G., & Shane, H. C. (1994). Science, reason, and facilitated communication. *Journal of the Association for Persons with Severe Handicaps, 19,* 157–172.

Gurry, S. E., & Larkin, A. S. (1999). Literacy learning abilities of children with developmental disabilities: What do we know? *Currents in literacy.* Retrieved June 17, 2003, from http://www.lesley.edu/academic_centers/hood/currents/v2n1/gurrylarkin.html

Halle, J. W., Chadsey, J., Lee, S., & Renzaglia, A. (2004). Systematic instruction. In C. H. Kennedy & E. M. Horn (Eds.), *Including students with severe disabilities* (pp. 54–77). Boston: Allyn & Bacon.

Harding, J. (2003). Spotlight on assistive technology. *Deaf-Blind Perspectives, 11*(1), 5–6.

Harris, T. L., & Hodges, R. E. (Eds.). (1995). *The literacy dictionary: The vocabulary of reading and writing.* Newark, DE: International Reading Assessment.

Hedberg, N. L., & Westberg, C. E. (1993). *Analyzing fictional narrative telling skills: Theory to practice.* Tucson, AZ: Communication Skill Builders.

Heller, K. W., Fredrick, L., Dykes, M. K., Best, S., & Cohen, E. (1999). A national perspective of competencies for teachers of individuals with physical and health disabilities. *Exceptional Children, 65,* 219–234.

Hodgdon, L. (1995). Visual strategies for improving communication. *Augmentative and Alternative Communication, 16,* 180–185. Troy, MI: Quirk Roberts.

Huer, M. B. (2000). Examining perceptions of graphic symbols across cultures: Preliminary study of the impact of culture/ethnicity. *Augmentative and Alternative Communication, 16,* 180–185.

Hunt, P., & Goetz, L. (1997). Research on inclusive educational programs, practices, and outcomes for students with severe disabilities. *The Journal of Special Education, 31*, 3–29.

Hunt, P., Soto, G., Maier, J., & Doering, K. (2003). Collaborative teaming to support students at risk and students with severe disabilities in general education classrooms. *Exceptional Children, 69*, 315–332.

Janney, R., & Snell, M. E. (2000). *Modifying schoolwork.* Baltimore: Paul H. Brookes.

Joseph, L. M., & Seery, M. E. (2004). Where is the phonics? A review of the literature on the use of phonetic analysis with students with mental retardation. *Remedial and Special Education, 25*, 88–94.

Justice, L. M., & Pullen, P. C. (2003). Promising interventions for promoting emergent literacy skills: Three evidence-based approaches. *Topics in Early Childhood Special Education, 23*, 99–113.

Kalyanpur, M., Harry, B., & Skrtic, T. (2000). Equity and advocacy: Expectations of culturally diverse families' participation in special education. *International Journal of Disability, Development and Education, 47*, 119–136.

Katims, D. S. (2000). Literacy instruction for people with mental retardation: Historical highlights and contemporary analysis. *Education and Training in Mental Retardation and Developmental Disabilities, 35*, 3–15.

Katims, D. S. (2001). Literacy assessment of students with mental retardation: An exploratory investigation. *Education and Training in Mental Retardation and Developmental Disabilities, 36*, 363–372.

Katz, J. R. (2001). Playing at home: The talk of pretend play. In D. K. Dickinson & P. O. Tabors (Eds.), *Beginning literacy with language* (pp. 53–73). Baltimore: Paul H. Brookes.

Keefe, E. B., Moore, V., & Duff, F. (2004). The four "knows" of collaborative teaching. *TEACHING Exceptional Children, 36*(5), 36–42.

Kimball, J. W., Kinney, E. M., Taylor, B. A., & Stromer, R. (2003). Lights, camera, action! Using engaging computer-cued activity schedules. *TEACHING Exceptional Children, 36*(1), 40–45.

Kleinert, H. L., Haigh, J., Kearns, J. F., & Kennedy, S. (2000). Alternate assessments: Lessons learned and roads to be taken. *Exceptional Children, 67*, 51–66.

Kleinert, H. L., & Kearns, J. F. (1999). A validation study of the performance indicators and learner outcomes of Kentucky's alternate assessment for students with significant disabilities. *Journal of the Association for Persons with Severe Handicaps, 24*, 100–110.

Kleinert, H. L., & Kearns, J. F. (2004). Alternate assessments. In F. P. Orelove, D., Sobsey, & R. K. Silberman (Eds.), *Educating children with multiple disabilities: A collaborative approach* (4th ed., pp. 115–150). Baltimore: Paul H. Brookes.

Kliewer, C. (1995). Young children's communication and literacy: A qualitative study of language in the inclusive preschool. *Mental Retardation, 33*, 143–152.

Kliewer, C. (1998). Citizenship in the literate community: An ethnography of children with Down syndrome and the written word. *Exceptional Children, 64,* 167–180.

Kliewer, C., & Biklen, D. (2001). "School's not really a place for reading": A research synthesis of the literate lives of students with severe disabilities. *Journal of the Association for Persons with Severe Handicaps, 26,* 1–12.

Kliewer, C., & Landis, D. (1999). Individualizing literacy instruction for young children with moderate to severe disabilities. *Exceptional Children, 66,* 85–100.

Koenig, A. J., & Farrenkopf, C. (1997). Essential experiences to undergird the early development of literacy. *Journal of Visual Impairment and Blindness, 91*(1), 14–25.

Koppenhaver, D. A. (2000). Literacy in AAC: What should be written on the envelope we push? *Augmentative and Alternative Communication, 16,* 270–279.

Koppenhaver, D. A., & Erickson, K. A. (1998). *Technologies to support reading comprehension in children with disabilities.* Center for Literacy and Disability Studies. Posted February 24, 1998, at http://www.surgy.mc.duke.edu/commdis/clds

Koppenhaver, D. A., Erickson, K. A., & Skotko, B. G. (2001). Supporting communication of girls with Rett syndrome and their mothers in storybook reading. *International Journal of Disabilities, Development, and Education, 48,* 395–410.

Kovach, T. M., & Kenyon, P. B. (2003). Visual issues and access to AAC. In J. C. Light, D. R. Beukelman, & J. Reichle (Eds.), *Communicative competence for individuals who use AAC: From research to effective practice* (pp. 277–319). Baltimore: Paul H. Brookes.

Kroeger, S., Burton, C., Comarata, A., Combs, C., Hamm, C., Hopkins, R., et al. (2004). Student voice and critical reflection: Helping students at risk. *TEACHING Exceptional Children, 36*(3), 50–57.

Lake, J. F., & Billingsley, B. S. (2000). An analysis of factors that contribute to parent-school conflict in special education. *Remedial and Special Education, 21,* 240–251.

Lalli, J. S., & Browder, D. M. (1993). Comparison of sight word training procedures with validation of the most practical procedures in teaching reading for daily living. *Research in Developmental Disabilities, 14,* 107–127.

Lewis, S., & Tolla, J. (2003). Creating and using tactile experience books for young children with visual impairments. *TEACHING Exceptional Children, 35*(1), 22–28.

Light, J., & Kelford Smith, A. (1993). The home literacy experiences of preschoolers who use augmentative communication systems and their nondisabled peers. *Augmentative and Alternative Communication, 9,* 10–25.

Locke, P. A., & Butterfield, R. (1998, November 19). *Promoting literacy for individuals with severe to moderate disabilities.* Retrieved June 12, 2003, from http://www.dinf.ne.jp/doc/english/Us_Eu/conf/csun_99/session0038.html

Logan, K. R., & Malone, D. M. (1998). Instructional contexts for students with moderate, severe, and profound intellectual disabilities in general education classrooms. *Education and Training in Mental Retardation and Developmental Disabilities, 33*, 62–75.

Lohrmann-O'Rourke, S., & Browder, D. M. (1998). Empirically based methods to assess the preferences of individuals with severe disabilities. *American Journal of Mental Retardation, 103*, 146–161.

Mainger, R. W., Deshler, D., Coleman, M. R., Kozleski, E., & Rodriguez-Walling, M. (2003). To ensure the learning of every child with a disability. *Focus on Exceptional Children, 35*(5), 1–12.

Marvin, C. (1994). Home literacy experiences of preschool children with single and multiple disorder. *Topics in Early Childhood Special Education, 14*, 436–454.

Mather, N., & Lachowicz, B. L. (1992). Shared writing: An instructional approach for reluctant writers. *TEACHING Exceptional Children, 25*(1), 26–30.

McEwen, I. R. (1997). Seating, other positioning and motor control. In L. Lloyed, D. Fuller, & H. Arvidson (Eds.), *Augmentative and alternative communication: A handbook of principles and practices* (pp. 280–298). Needham Heights, MA: Allyn & Bacon.

McSheehan, M., Sonnenmeier, R., & Jorgensen, C. M. (2002, May). Communication and learning: Creating systems of support for students with significant disabilities. *TASH Connections*, 8–13.

Miles, B. (1999). *Talking the language of the hands to the hands.* Monmouth, OR: DBLINK, The National Information Clearinghouse on Children Who Are Deaf-Blind. (ERIC Document Reproduction Service No. ED 419–331)

Mirenda, P. (1993). AAC: Bonding the uncertain mosaic. *Augmentative and Alternative Communication, 9*, 3–9.

Mirenda, P., & Erickson, K. A. (2000). Augmentative communication and literacy. In A. M. Wetherby & B. M. Prizant (Eds.), *Autism spectrum disorders: A transactional developmental perspective* (pp. 333–367). Baltimore: Paul H. Brookes.

Moes, D. R. (1998). Integrating choice-making opportunities within teacher-assigned academic tasks to facilitate the performance of children with autism. *Journal of the Association for Persons with Severe Handicaps, 23*, 319–328.

Musselwhite, C., & King De-Baun, P. (1997). *Emerging literacy success: Merging whole language and teaching for students with disabilities.* Park City, UT: Creative Communicating.

Neuman, S. B. (1999). Creating continuity in early literacy: Linking home and school with a culturally responsive approach. In L. B. Gambreel, L. M. Morrow, S. B. Neuman, & M. Pressley (Eds.), *Best practices in literacy instruction* (pp. 258–270). New York: Guilford Press.

No Child Left Behind Act of 2001. (2002). Pub. L. No. 107–110, 115 Stat.1425.

Ohtake, Y., Santos, R. M., & Fowler, S. A. (2000). It's a three-way conversation: Families, service providers and interpreters working together. *Young Exceptional Children, 4*, 12–18.

Ollila, L. O., & Mayfield, M. I. (1992). Home and school together: Helping beginning readers to succeed. In S. I. Samuals & A. E. Farstrup (Eds.), *What research has to say about reading instruction* (2nd ed., pp. 17–45). Newark, DE: International Reading Assessment.

Parette, P., Chang, S. L., & Huer, M. B. (2004). First generation Chinese American families' attitudes regarding disabilities and educational interventions. *Focus on Autism and Other Developmental Disabilities, 19,* 114–123.

Raver, S. A. (2004). Monitoring child progress in early childhood special education settings. *TEACHING Exceptional Children, 36*(6), 52–57.

Reichle, J., Hidecker, M. J. C., Brady, N. C., & Terry, N. (2004). Intervention strategies for communication: Using aided augmentative communication systems. In J. C. Light, D. R. Beukelman, & J. Reichle (Eds.), *Communicative competence for individuals who use AAC: From research to effective practice* (pp. 441–478). Baltimore: Paul H. Brookes.

Romski, M. A., & Sevcik, R. A. (1996). *Breaking the speech barrier: Language development through augmented means.* Baltimore: Paul H. Brookes.

Rossi, P. J. (2000). Many ways in the way: Supporting the languages and literacies of culturally, linguistically, and developmentally diverse children. In T. Fletcher & C. Bos (Eds.), *Helping individuals with disabilities and their families: Mexican and U.S. perspectives* (pp. 171–187). Tempe, AZ: Bilingual Review Press.

Rowland, C., & Schweigert, P. (1993). Analyzing the communication environment to increase functional communication. *Journal of the Association for Persons with Severe Handicaps, 18,* 161–176.

Ryndak, D. L., & Fisher, D. (Eds.). (2003). *The foundations of inclusive education: A compendium of articles on effective strategies to achieve inclusive education* (2nd ed.). Baltimore: TASH.

Ryndak, D. L., Morrison, A. P., & Sommerstein, L. (1999). Literacy before and after inclusion in general education settings: A case study. *Journal of the Association for Persons with Severe Handicaps, 24,* 5–22.

Schlosser, R. W. (2003). Roles of speech output in augmentative and alternative communication: Narrative review. *Augmentative and Alternative Communication, 19,* 5–27.

Schmidt, J., Alper, S., Raschke, D., & Ryndak, D. (2000). Effects of using a photographic cueing package during routine school transitions with a child who has autism. *Mental Retardation, 38,* 131–137.

Siegel-Causey, E., & Allinder, R. M. (1998). Using alternate assessment for students with severe disabilities: Alignment with best practices. *Education and Training in Mental Retardation and Developmental Disabilities, 33,* 168–178.

Sigafoos, J., Didden, R., & O'Reilly, M. (2003). Effects of speech output on maintenance of requesting and frequency of vocalizations in three children with developmental disabilities. *Augmentative and Alternative Communication, 19,* 37–47.

Sigafoos, J., & Mirenda, P. (2002). Strengthening communicative behaviors for gaining access to desired items and activities. In J. Reichle, D. R. Beukelman, & J. C. Light (Eds.), *Exemplary practices for beginning communicators: Implications for AAC* (pp. 123–156). Baltimore: Paul H. Brookes.

Smith, R. L., Collins, B. C., Schuster, J. W., & Kleinert, H. (1999). Teaching table cleaning skills to secondary students with moderate/severe disabilities: Facilitating observational learning during instructional downtime. *Education and Training in Mental Retardation and Developmental Disabilities, 34*, 342–353.

Snell, M. E. (2002). Using dynamic assessment with learners who communicate nonsymbolically. *Augmentative and Alternative Communication, 18*, 163–176.

Stromer, R., Mackay, H. A., Howell, S. R., & McVay, A. A. (1996). Teaching computer-assisted spelling to individuals with developmental and hearing disabilities: Transfer of stimulus control to writing task. *Journal of Applied Behavior Analysis, 29*, 25–42.

Sulzby, E. (1994). Children's emergent reading of favorite story books: A developmental study. In R. B. Ruddell, M. R. Ruddell, & H. Singer (Eds.), *Theoretical models and processes of reading* (4th ed., pp. 244–280). Newark, DE: International Reading Association.

Sulzby, E., & Teale, W. H. (1991). Emergent literacy. In R. Barr, M. L. Kamil, P. Mosenthal, & P. D. Pearson (Eds.), *Handbook of reading research* (Vol. 2, pp. 727–757). White Plains, NY: Longman.

Swartz, M. K., & Hendricks, C. G. (2000). Factors that influence the book selection process of students with special needs. *Journal of Adolescent and Adult Literacy, 43*, 608–618.

Taylor, R. L. (2003). *Assessment of exceptional students: Educational and psychological procedures* (6th ed.). Boston: Allyn & Bacon.

Thompson, S. J., Quenemoen, R. F., Thurlow, M. L., & Ysseldyke, J. E. (2001). *Alternate assessments for students with disabilities.* Thousand Oaks, CA: Corwin Press and Council for Exceptional Children.

Tindal, G., McDonald, M., Tedesco, M., Glasgow, A., Almond, P., Crawford, L., et al. (2003). Alternative assessment in reading and math: Development and validation for students with significant disabilities. *Exceptional Children, 69*, 481–494.

Turnbull, A., & Turnbull, R. (2001). Self-determination for individuals with significant cognitive disabilities and their families. *Journal of the Association for Persons With Severe Handicaps, 26*, 56–62.

Utley, B. L., & Rapport, M. J. K. (2000). Exploring role release in the multidisciplinary team. *Physical Disabilities: Education and Related Services, XVIII*, 89–118.

Wehmeyer, M. L. (1999). Assistive technology and students with mental retardation: Utilization and barriers. *Journal of Special Education Technology, 14*(1), 48–58.

Wehmeyer, M. L. (2003). Defining mental retardation and ensuring access to the general curriculum. *Education and Training in Developmental Disabilities, 38*, 271–283.

Wehmeyer, M. L., Lattin, D., Lapp-Rincker, G., & Agran, M. (2003). Access to the general curriculum of middle-school students with mental retardation: An observational study. *Remedial and Special Education, 24*, 262–272.

Wehmeyer, M. L., & Metzler, C. A. (1995). How self-determined are people with mental retardation? The national consumer survey. *Mental Retardation, 33*, 111–119.

Westling, D. L., & Fox, L. (2000). *Teaching students with severe disabilities* (2nd ed.). Upper Saddle River, NJ: Prentice Hall.

White, M. T., Garrett, B., Kearns, J. F., & Grisham-Brown, J. (2003). Instruction and assessment: How students with deaf-blindness fare in large-scale alternate assessments. *Research and Practice for Persons with Severe Disabilities, 28*, 205–213.

Williamson, G. G., & Anzalone, M. (2001). *Sensory integration and self-regulation in infants and toddlers: Helping very young children interact with their environment.* Washington, DC: Zero to Three.

Wood, L. A., Lasker, J., Siegel-Causey, E., Beukelman, D. R., & Ball, L. (1998). Input framework for augmentative and alternative communication. *Augmentative and Alternative Communication, 14*, 261–267.

List of Tables

List of Figures

Index

Page references followed by *fig* indicate an illustrated figure; followed by *t* indicates a table.

**CORWIN
PRESS**

The Corwin Press logo—a raven striding across an open book—represents the union of courage and learning. Corwin Press is committed to improving education for all learners by publishing books and other professional development resources for those serving the field of K–12 education. By providing practical, hands-on materials, Corwin Press continues to carry out the promise of its motto: **"Helping Educators Do Their Work Better."**

Printed in the United States
94639LV00003BA/22/A

9 780761 988786